Letting go - taking hold

A guide to independent language learning by teachers for teachers

edited by

Brian Page

The views expressed in this book are those of the editor and contributors and do not necessarily reflect the views of CILT.

First published 1992
Copyright © 1992 Centre for Information on Language Teaching and Research
ISBN 1 874016 25 9

Cover by Logos Design & Advertising
Printed in Great Britain by Blackmore Press

Published by Centre for Information on Language Teaching and Research, Regent's College, Inner Circle, Regent's Park, London NW1 4NS.

CONTENTS

Acknowledgements

As editor, I want to express my deepest gratitude first to the planning group who have steered this work to publication:

Stephanie Buchanan, CILT
Ian Gathercole, Resources for Learning Development Unit, Bristol
Vee Harris, Goldsmiths' College, London
Ute Hitchin, CILT
Bernardette Holmes, Modern Languages Inspector, Essex
Lid King, CILT
Christiane Montlibert, The Boswells Comprehensive School, Chelmsford
Alan Moys, CILT

then to the teachers who have written sections specifically for the book and who are mentioned at the appropriate point; to the dozens of teachers whose ideas gleaned from countless conversations are reflected here and, not least, to the participants at Dyffryn House who cheerfully laboured from early morning to late into the night working out ideas and setting them down. This book cannot do them justice.

However, the book should, I think, be dedicated to the learners who are the cause of it all. I do not think Christiane Montlibert's statement about them can be bettered:

These learners can do much more than we ask of them.

Brian Page
Leeds

Introduction

In January 1990 CILT organised a two-day conference on *Autonomy in Language Learning* at the Lane End conference centre in High Wycombe. The proceedings were subsequently published by CILT (*Autonomy in language learning*, edited by Ian Gathercole, CILT, 1990).

It was the unanimous wish of the participants that a follow-up workshop lasting more than two days if possible should be organised to explore the practical implications of all the ideas that emerged at Lane End. A four-day workshop was therefore held at Dyffryn House, Cardiff on 14-18 November 1990.

The main speakers were:

Richard Johnstone, University of Stirling - a pioneer in communicative language teaching, director of the team that produced *Tour de France* (Heinemann, 1981) and author of *Communicative interaction: a guide for language teachers* (CILT, 1989) - who spoke on autonomy and foreign language learning development.

Frances Morley, currently at Woking Sixth Form College and Roehampton Institute, who spoke on teaching cross-curricular themes through the foreign language.

Mel Austin, Deputy Head of George Ward Comprehensive School, Melksham, Wiltshire and a member of the National Curriculum Working Group for Modern Languages, who spoke on learner autonomy in the National Curriculum.

Throughout the four days we had seminars and commentaries on our work from **Leni Dam**, who had also spoken at the Lane End conference. Leni Dam is a foreign languages adviser for Greve, Denmark, teaches English and maths at primary and secondary level, and is an in-service teacher trainer at the Royal Danish School of Educational Studies. She has been involved in research projects at national and European level and is a coursebook writer and the author of many articles on autonomy.

Chapter 1

TOWARDS LEARNER INDEPENDENCE

The ultimate aim of teaching has always been to enable the learner to do without the teacher. Unfortunately, we have often lost sight of this age-old objective. Teachers became the fount of all knowledge, learners sat at their feet and became dependent. How learners were to manage once they had left was not the teacher's concern. When it became apparent that this was not particularly effective, the method was modified. Teachers began to make things easier for the learner by presenting predigested material in an 'accessible' form - *the layers of support that well-intentioned teachers give to learners,* as Richard Johnstone has put it. In language learning this usually meant textbooks written by English speakers leading to examinations set by English speakers. It was the usual experience for a learner never to meet an example of genuine foreign language produced by a native speaker in the whole of a five-year course in secondary school. All was abridged, amended or specially concocted to be accessible to the learner.

In recent years we have moved towards providing examples of authentic foreign language for learners to work with - signs, brochures, extracts from magazines and newspapers, genuine French/German/Spanish people recorded on audio and video tape. But we still tend in textbooks and in class to give a great deal of support - word lists, explanations, and questions that point learners in the direction we want them to go. How else, we say, will they be able to cope with genuine foreign language? But if we as teachers are to do our job properly, we must give them the means to cope on their own.

How can we do this? How can we enable learners to function independently when the teacher is no longer there? And that means that learners must not only be able to use their skills on their own but also add to them, refine them and expand their knowledge on their own. In other words, as well as a basic communicative competence in the foreign language we must give learners the skills to study by themselves, experience in independent working, strategies for adding to their repertoire, knowledge of tools like dictionaries and reference grammars that they can use for themselves and, above all, the confidence to go on working on their own. How can we begin to give learners the independence needed for all this? More important still, how can we teach learners to be and feel more independent, to take more conscious responsibility for their own learning? To show how this can be done in the case of foreign language learning is the purpose of this book.

Three things help.

1. Our awareness that teachers can teach as much as they like but only learners learn. We all know this. The ability of some learners to gain little from us over a long period and in spite of our best efforts is amazing. So perhaps we should concern ourselves as much with making learners efficient learners as we do with making ourselves efficient teachers.

2. There has been a general movement towards systems that give more independence to learners in schools. This is not only because it makes them more efficient as learners of whatever the subject happens to be. It also has much broader educational effects in making adolescents aware of how to make choices, the effects of their actions, their responsibility for their own learning, how to collaborate with others in group projects, how to present findings for an outside audience; in other words, how to learn. All of these are important life skills.

3. The National Curriculum will have an effect. The Statutory Order includes the following section (page 26):

Developing the ability to learn independently

Links with:

In learning and using the target language, pupils should have regular opportunities to:

- work independently of the teacher (on their own and with others);

- use a range of reference materials and resources (*eg glossaries, exercise books, textbooks, bilingual and monolingual dictionaries, indexes, encyclopaedias*);

AT 1, 2, 3, 4

- use computers (*eg for language games, problem-solving, information retrieval, word-processing, drafting and redrafting, desktop publishing and communicating via electronic mail*);

- develop independence in their choice of tasks, materials, and use of equipment (*eg audio and video recorders and video cameras*).

There is another reason which is just as important. All the evidence suggests that giving learners a degree of independence, a degree of control over what, how and when they learn, increases the efficiency of their learning. If they are given the chance to understand the constraints imposed by syllabuses, examinations and availability of materials, and, in negotiation with their teachers, work out for themselves what they want to do and how they intend to do it, then decide how well they achieved their objective, they learn more efficiently than if they are using imposed language to deal with imposed ideas.

So, for educational reasons, reasons of general efficiency, and in order to meet the National Curriculum requirements, ways have to be found to enable learners to become not only independent users of a foreign language but also independent improvers of their own skills and independent expanders of their own knowledge.

The techniques suggested in this book are all provided by practising teachers who have used them. They present a wide variety of approaches and different degrees of independence for learners. We hope that these experiences will have something positive to offer to all teachers of foreign languages in the United Kingdom, who work with many teaching styles and in greatly differing teaching circumstances.

Chapter 2

HOW WE GOT STARTED

Like M Jourdain speaking prose, many teachers are operating simple independent learning systems without realising it. When asked the question: *is it all that different?* Hilary Norris Evans[1] wrote:

> *Yes and no. Yes, if you enjoy total control over your class, like them learning quietly in rows and having mainly teacher-centred work. Yes, if you think of the process as teaching rather than learning. No, if your students work in pairs and groups quite a lot of the time and individual students and groups do different, differentiated and varying amounts of work. No, if they are allowed to use resources freely, although you do have some teacher-centred learning.*

The first steps, then, are not necessarily that far removed from what is being done already. For most people indeed it would be unwise to move suddenly from one teaching style to another. The principle to have in mind is that learners should be asked to take on more responsibility by making choices and doing things for themselves. This can happen in quite small ways and with quite traditional practices. For example:

● Many teachers still give ten words of vocabulary taken from the current work to be learnt for homework and tested. Not everyone thinks this is a useful practice but many do. It can be improved if you ask learners to choose for themselves ten words to learn. Next day, instead of the traditional test, the learners are given three minutes to write down as many of their words with English equivalents as they can. Other pupils then mark them by looking them up in the textbook to check. In the process they learn a few more words they hadn't chosen for themselves. The teacher should look briefly at the test papers to see the range of words chosen; to check that the potentially lazy don't choose a string of simple words they already know (this rarely happens) and that the marking is accurate. The whole thing takes no more time than the traditional format and the results tend to be more lasting because the learners were personally involved in what they were doing.

---

[1] See her notes on pages 21 and 23

- If you do exercises from the textbook orally round the class, don't just go from one to ten, let each learner choose which one to have a go at. Learners usually choose one they can do as opposed to being obliged to try one they can't. This is a distinct advantage as there is no point in forcing people to make mistakes. It also shows the teacher clearly where the class has difficulties - it's the sentence no-one chooses to do. If setting exercises to do in class or for homework, it is often possible to offer two or three to choose from rather than asking all the class to do the same one. If they then have to mark each other's before you see them they are doing two exercises anyway.

- If you have a series of comprehension questions on a passage, let learners produce two or three questions of their own for the rest of the class to answer as well as or instead of doing those provided by the book.

These are modest beginnings starting from very traditional practices, but they are undoubtedly first steps in making learners more responsible for what they learn and therefore more efficient learners. Above all, don't expect anything to work particularly well first time. Learners have to get used to exercising independence just as teachers have to get used to giving it. Teachers have to let go and learners have to take hold, and both may need to learn how to do it.

What follows in this chapter are the experiences of a number of teachers taking their first steps in providing more autonomy for their pupils. The experience is very diverse and sometimes inconsistent. What works in one school with one teacher will not necessarily do so in the same way in another. The degree of autonomy or the interpretation of what the word means in practice varies. What is common to all the experiences, however, is an effort on the part of the teachers to move some responsibility from themselves to the learners and, most important of all, the positive outcome - the learners learn more efficiently. It all worked well enough for the teachers to want to go on and refine and develop their ideas and practices.

Schools

Vee Harris
Goldsmiths' College,
London

Vee Harris, a lecturer at Goldsmiths' College and a former secondary school teacher who continues to work very closely with teachers in schools, suggests breaking down the change in teaching style into manageable steps. She draws her examples from the work of teachers she knows.

Step 1: Some pair and group work

Learners do in pairs/groups an exercise you might have done altogether in class. Extend by having two activities; one half of the class does one, the other does the other.

★ This gets the learners used to being in pairs/groups while not seeing it as a chance to misbehave, but it has no real element of choice or responsibility. Responsibility is limited to the time learners are in the group.

Step 2: Carousel

Have a menu of activities. Learners do all or some of them. Extend to doing the carousel over two lessons, not just one.

★ One of the problems of this approach is that it can be very purposeless, a bit of reading, speaking, etc but where is it all going? This type of carousel is better if there is a purpose - all activities are connected with one topic for example.

Step 3: An alternative or extra step

Split the textbook into units which can correspond to chapters or can be smaller sections. Give deadlines for when each unit has to be completed but say that the learners can tackle the exercises in any order, including what they do for homework. Some additional tasks for the more able - often around grammar or writing - can be added. Learners tick a checklist when they complete a unit and the teacher checks. The checklist should have space for a note of oral progress (by the foreign language assistant if you have one).

★ This system relies on the quality of the coursebook and doesn't get pupils used to using a range of resources.

Step 4: Resources

The teacher draws up a list of all the resources around the GCSE topics. Alison Orr (see page 10) devised activity sheets to go with each topic. In her classroom are all the resources needed for the topic plus a folder. In the folder are all the activity sheets, self-marking cards, any extra grammar summaries, any games to be played around the topic, etc. Pupils can help themselves and be referred to the resources they need.

★ The advantage is that this is more economical and uses a range of resources, but the problem is that it is still the teacher who decides what is to be done.

Step 5: Learners' programmes

Steven Fawkes (see page 18) arranged a system for his learners after their mock GCSE exams. He drew up a list of resources and put them on a database, but pupils were then free to decide what they needed to work on, e.g. speaking at the campsite, and were referred to a range of resources (listening, speaking cards, etc) for that particular need. So the learners themselves determine their own programme according to their strengths and weaknesses. They keep a track of this using their own personal diaries where they have to mark what reading, listening, speaking and writing they have done, what vocabulary and grammar, and what they need to work on still.

**Bridget Barling
Broomfields School,
Southgate**

Bridget Barling started with homework only, just to see how it would go. Here is her diary.

January

As I didn't want chaos in the classroom, I decided to start with homework. I made as comprehensive a list as possible (see page 9) for pupils to make their choices. I must admit it did seem like a miracle in the beginning. Pupils were enthusiastic, choosing their preferred task (some of them spending hours on the work). For me, the most exciting homeworks that came back were conversations on tapes with brothers, sisters, parents, aunts, uncles, friends. There were those, of course, who went for the *mots cachés* every time (until redirected). But it worked. I have since made lists of what to say in postcards or letters for those who need their imaginations jogged.

October

In July a large needlework room had been vacated, so I had grabbed it, having fallen for the dozen sockets mounted on special tables. I am losing the room this year and hope that I can adapt what I have been doing to the smaller room.

**What I have
been doing**

I made task sheets for the class (handwritten bandas). About a dozen tasks - listening, reading, listening and reading together, writing and speaking. Pupils kept their task sheets in their files so that at the beginning of each lesson they could continue where they had left off. If they wanted to do something different from what was on the task sheet they could.

We went through the first task sheet to make sure it was clear to everyone. They could do what they liked, i.e. in any order. It just took off from there. Of course I did point out that they were doing 'their own thing'.

**Organisation of
materials and
furniture**

Either in groups or old-fashioned rows. It doesn't seem to make much difference. I have had both. What does seem important to me is that there is some kind of shelving around the room or tables strategically placed for housing materials. I have found the lids of duplicating paper boxes or the boxes themselves cut down very useful, even necessary, for keeping the materials in. Empty shoe boxes or the four-tier wire mesh wall racks from *Homebase* are ideal for housing the tapes.

I did it my way and I have a feeling it was the wrong way. I jumped in at the deep end. I started with all classes, all years. Because pupils are working at different speeds you have to be way out in front with task sheets, banda sheets with questions for the reading and listening tasks, and answer cards. I think I was too ambitious doing a tailor-made job for each class. Perhaps it will be easier when I start using a variety of books (textbooks and others) and use their material. The trouble is you find you want to ask more questions on a listening or reading text than are given. Answer sheets have to be made if pupils are working at their own speed.

Les devoirs

N'oubliez pas de mettre (en français) la date, le temps, l'heure et où tu es!

Cette semaine je vais . . . .

- ☐ décrire une image
- ☐ dessiner et décrire une image
- ☐ apprendre un poème
- ☐ apprendre des mots (écrivez les mots)
- ☐ apprendre les numéros (écrivez les numéros)
- ☐ écrire des phrases ou une petite histoire (écrivez un titre)
- ☐ écrire une conversation (un titre 'au café', 'dans la rue', 'à la gare', etc)
- ☐ enregistrer une conversation (au téléphone, dans un magasin, à l'hôtel, etc)
- ☐ lire et je vais enregistrer ma voix sur cassette
- ☐ lire Bibliobus et je vais faire les activités
- ☐ lire un livre (mettez lequel) et je vais en faire un résumé
- ☐ faire un peu de géographie et écrire quelques mots la-dessus
- ☐ écrire une carte postale
- ☐ écrire une lettre (en utilisant tu ... ou ... en utilisant vous)
     (demandez au prof si vous n'avez pas des idées)
- ☐ faire un 'mots cachés' (minimum 30 mots)
- ☐ décrire quelqu'un (une personne célèbre, un prof, un/e ami/e, ma mère, etc)
- ☐ faire une devinette
- ☐ faire un dessin animé avec paroles
- ☐ écrire une description de quelque chose ou d'une scène pour être dessiner
- ☐ faire un exercice de Tricolore à la page ...
- ☐ faire un peu de grammaire sur ... (demandez au prof)
- ☐ faire et remplir une formule
- ☐ faire un menu
- ☐ décrire ma maison, ma rue, les environs
- ☐ décrire ma journée (à l'école, à la maison)
- ☐ écrire mon journal
- ☐ écrire quelque chose sur le calendrier
- ☐ lire 'La fueille française' et faire les devinettes etc
- ☐ décrire mes vacances
- ☐ enregistrer la météo pour la France

D'autres possibilités (Si vous préférez enregistrer - allez-y!) . . . .

   . . . .

   . . . .

I was always worried that I would never be able to cope with pupils doing a variety of activities at the same time. Well, I have coped. And it is tremendous to be able to have one-to-one conversations whilst the rest are busying away. But I do think there might have been less pressure had I started with one year group and not tried to cover all years. Of course you do get those who shoot ahead and those who just amble along, but then I suppose this is part of their own autonomous nature showing up, and this does perhaps happen more often in our school as we are mixed ability all the way through.

I can't say my way is working as perfectly as I would wish it to - I need to do a lot of tidying up. For example, this year each class has had two, three or more non-English speakers and though autonomy should be the ideal answer for such a situation, without having the digestible food available for their particular learning, these pupils pose a problem for the teacher (no time to create material). I hope next year to produce the necessary stock of food so that these pupils may also dip into a little learning. The *Collins Pocket Dictionary* has been an absolute boon in the classroom. I have managed to get twelve per class. Pupils who didn't even know how to use a dictionary actually pick them up as they come into the room. It's a pleasure to see.

This, of course, is not total autonomy, but even the birds are restricted.

Alison Orr
Whitefields School,
Cricklewood

How you start depends a lot on how the pupils have been learning previously, how confident and comfortable the teacher feels about a different approach, and the amount of work required to adapt existing schemes of work. It's so much easier if you have colleagues who will share the workload and the ideas and mistakes.

I personally don't think that you need to say anything to start with to the class. If you have pupils who are used to working in pairs/groups and are not teacher-dominated all of the time, then you are just building on this. If not, it's best to start with pair and group work (see Vee Harris' contribution on page 6). For my pupils the biggest and nicest surprise was when I told them they could use the cassette player and headphones and spend as much time as they wanted on the listening. I think that each teacher has to decide for him/herself what needs to be said, and if the pupils are not used to any sort of collaborative working, then the teacher will have to introduce a new approach gradually.

In terms of language content, it is the same as before I started independent learning. I am using the same materials; I have just adapted them for a different style of learning.

Materials

My year 10 and 11 pupils in French and German are given a task sheet for the assignment we are working on. This task sheet tells them (in French or German) what they have to do and which textbooks or worksheets they will need to use. The pupils keep the task sheet in their A4 folder and tick off each task as it is done. I have an A4 sheet of paper with the names of the pupils and the numbers of the tasks on it. The pupils have to tick this sheet during each lesson to indicate what they have done. I collect all folders for marking once a week. Each assignment belongs to a term of work which is colour-coded, e.g. the first term is related to making contact with your penfriend, all assignments are in pink folders and the task sheets are on pink card. Colour-coding helps me to keep things in order. All answer cards are on white card. It is also essential that everything has a title and a number.

Years 7 to 9 do not have access to quite so many resources and we tend to stick to one main coursebook with lots of home-made worksheets and games. These pupils are not given a task sheet. They are told each lesson what the aims are and what has to be completed.

You have to be organised, otherwise everything will get into a muddle. You also need a table (I use my own desk) where the answer cards, worksheets, books, etc are placed and pupils come and help themselves. It takes a lot of persuasion to get some pupils to take things from my desk without asking first.

Tables need to be grouped so that pupils are sitting in groups of four or six. It is essential that you have your own classroom, but if you are moving around then pupils need lessons in moving furniture quietly. An OHP is invaluable. It is almost impossible to include listening tasks if you don't have cassette players with headphones. A good extension lead is essential if you only have one or two power points in the classroom. Make the classroom into a bright cheerful resource area. Have around the room phrases in French/German/English etc that they will need to use, e.g. *j'ai oublié mon cahier*. Have up on the walls vocabulary relevant to what they are doing, and work done by the pupils.

Furniture

I am certainly not one of those people who jump on bandwagons just because something is new. In fact, in common with many modern linguists, I suppose I've become a little cynical over the years with regard to the string of 'cures' produced for all our classroom ills. However, I would also admit that teaching languages to everybody, although philosophically very justifiable, is not the easiest of challenges to succeed in and I personally felt dissatisfied on many occasions with my ability to get the message across to all pupils, despite my own enthusiasm. It was at this point that I became aware of the potential of flexible learning and so duly went along to a course run by CILT on autonomous learning that promised to challenge some of my thinking on language teaching. This course, and its subsequent follow-up, has indeed had a radical effect on my perception of what my role as a languages teacher in the classroom really might be. I was forced to re-examine my own aims and objectives and was permitted glimpses of some really exciting things going on in other parts of the country. I felt that, unlike most courses, here I had been presented with a new approach that really enthused me and created a desire to start experimenting, despite the current pressures.

Martyn Glass
Roade School,
Northants

In a nutshell, the main thrust of the argument was that pupils will respond better and learn more thoroughly if they are much more involved in their own learning process. If they have a say in what they learn and how they learn it, and if they realise why they are learning in a particular way, then they are going to tackle the task more enthusiastically. Motivation and involvement are increased and so, as a consequence, is enjoyment. Some of you will doubtless have recognised that increasing responsibility in the learning process is a fundamental concept in the National Curriculum document, but many will be asking how it can be turned into a practical reality. Let me give you three concrete examples from my own teaching this year. I have continued working with traditional textbooks but have attempted to make use of them in a rather different way. Pupils sit in groups of six so that furniture does not need to be moved when group work gets underway.

Example 1

Year 10 French group. Average and above average ability.
Textbook: *Tricolore 4A*. Course: MEG GCSE.

Unit 2 on 'Holiday accommodation' was tackled like this:

1. Brainstorming about different types of accommodation.

2. Setting ourselves an aim for the unit. It was decided that each group (tables of four to six pupils) would devise a project illustrating both the subject matter and the new grammar to be put together at the end of the unit.

3. We tackled the major sections of the unit, sometimes together as a class (usually introduction of new material), more often in small groups, each working on different skills, following a series of worksheets which contained a range of graded tasks in each skill.

4. Three lessons (each one hour) and two homeworks were devoted to the projects. They mostly consisted of a documented visit to France with itineraries, postcards, diaries, taped dialogues, brochures and plans, all drawn up in French by the groups. They shared out different aspects of the work and then brought it all together in booklet/display/package format.

All four stages were conducted throughout in French although the pupils often discussed what they were doing amongst themselves in English.

We are now in the middle of Unit 3 on 'Transport'. This time each group has chosen a different method of transport to study in depth. At the end of this they will present their findings to all the other groups in the form of a presentation, by means of OHTs, plays or some other form that they devise.

Example 2

Year 11 French group. Below average to very below average.
Textbook: *Hexagone +*. Course: SEG Modular.

1. Module 4 'Leisure'. Each pupil was issued with a pack of assignments (produced by SEG), each one graded (levels 1-4).

2. Each pupil plotted his/her own way through the assignments with 'helpsheets' (prepared by me) to assist them in practising the necessary skills and acquiring vocabulary for tackling each task.

3. Very little 'up-front' teaching. I constantly circulated, helping individuals as and when they requested help - and to make sure that everyone was actually working. Each pupil proceeded at his/her own pace.

4. Assignments within the module had a logical progression based on a work simulation situation. (The pupils perceive this as 'different' and 'more interesting'.) A time limit was set for completion and pupils were encouraged to try as many assignments as possible.

Year 9 German group. Mixed ability.   **Example 3**
Textbook: *Deutsch Heute 1*. Topic: Youth hostelling.

1. Brainstorming: reasons for going to Germany, how to get there, where to stay, comparisons between different sorts of accommodation, etc. Youth hostelling was chosen because little was known about it.

2. Discussion of how to go about a holiday of that type.

3. Working through each stage of the planning, the journey, the arrival, the youth hostel itself, in a natural order, choosing the appropriate sections of *Deutsch Heute* as the pupils needed them (mostly group work).

4. The holiday was simulated - with appropriate letters being sent off and bookings made.

Again, all aspects of the above were carried out in German.

Perhaps there is nothing earth-shattering in the examples I have cited, but I feel that I have approached each unit of work afresh, seeking to find a way of representing the topic in a way that will catch the pupils' imagination and get them involved to the maximum in every aspect of what they are doing. Some ideas have worked better than others, some groups have responded better than others, but I feel, personally, that an enormous weight has been taken off my shoulders. I am no longer expecting their progress to be totally dependent on my 'performance' at the front of the class. They have taken on board more responsibility for their own progress and my role is much more that of initiator and facilitator of activities, just one resource amongst many others. This has led to a greater feeling of success with all ability levels and a sense of satisfaction that pupils are benefiting from their lessons more than before. These ideas have been shared with the other members of the Faculty and most have taken on board some, if not most, of the underlying concepts. From a simple beginning the ripples in the pool are spreading outwards, and our pupils are becoming far more committed to languages and are deriving much more enjoyment from lessons. They are much less spectators and much more active participants in their learning experience.

Margaret Tumber
Alec Hunter
Comprehensive
School,
Braintree, Essex

Divide and rule?

This contribution will chronicle the stages through which one member of the language teaching profession passed on the journey from a wholly teacher-directed, full frontal approach to a situation where the learner assumes responsibility as an independent individual.

As with many other aspects of human progress, necessity was the mother of invention. It was 1973 in a newly re-organised, ex-secondary modern mixed comprehensive school in Essex. Faced with unsuitable materials and unwilling pupils, I realised that my own learning experience in the modern languages department of a grammar school was not going to provide an appropriate pattern for success here. Realisation that the needs of the learners were not being met forced me to look for alternatives to the whole class/coursebook cover-to-cover approach.

Control of a class of thirty disaffected fourteen-year-olds en masse was a problem. Even spells of 'silent' writing (copying, filling-in exercises) gave no guarantee of concentrated or worthwhile effort and the organisation of anything more active ran the risk of degenerating into chaos. The first step was to relinquish the confrontational stance between board and serried ranks of class and try an arrangement which was both physically and psychologically different. The class was divided in two. One half worked on 'background', on topics and with materials selected by the teacher, while the other half subdivided into two again. Each subgroup worked for half the lesson time with the teacher (or sometimes with the assistant) and for the other half-lesson continued work done with the teacher or prepared the work that would be done with this support. At this stage there was a high level of teacher direction - in the selection of the groups, the selection and provision of topics and materials, the arrangement of the furniture and the monitoring and checking of work. In a two-week cycle of two (50-minute) lessons per week, however, there was guaranteed teacher time for even the shyest individual and a framework for the containment of the more demanding elements in the class. Initially, this way of working was confined to 'difficult' third and fourth year groups (bottom sets), but in the years which followed was extended to include all classes and other teachers in the department.

Four-phase group work

The move to another school as head of department led to the development of a system in which all teachers in the department took part and which operated in a total mixed-ability setting where German was sole first foreign language. This matter of language was perhaps not without significance. On the one hand it highlighted the need for home production of materials - we were teaching right across the ability range from 11 to 16 - and it threw up no difficulties of pronunciation for pupils who met unfamiliar vocabulary when working in their group. The four phases represented the four skills - speaking, reading and understanding, listening and understanding, and writing - which would be tested at GCSE. Under topic area headings, groups completed tasks in each skill area in turn, so that four separate activities took place in the same room during the same lesson time, and work on a topic area culminated in an 'end of topic' test. The teacher was now completely mobile, though attention was centred on the speaking group where individuals performed role-play situations under each topic area and had their achievement recorded. Working in this way caused the department to produce much more 'custom-made' material, to work much more as a team in the production not only of pupil tasks but on answer sheets for these and extension tasks for the groups that finished early. Pupils clearly enjoyed working in their groups though some awkward combinations and uneven group sizes, together with those inconsistencies of length of time taken by groups to complete tasks resulted from the rigidity of the four-phase system. Certainly the teacher's role had begun to change from that of director to that of presenter and provider of support. There was scope now for learners to be involved in a less regimented way so that their needs could be addressed. Even in groups of thirty proceeding in lockstep, individuals do not progress at the same rate.

The progression outlined thus far will serve to show that change comes about as a result of perceived needs and that once the first steps are taken there is no turning back. With the experience described above behind me, the move to another school and another head of department post brought the daunting task of building on this past experience and at the same time beginning again with learners and colleagues who had had no part in the story so far. Would I start again from scratch 'in a small way' (just with my classes) or 'go the whole hog'? If making an honest attempt to meet the individual needs of each learner, and thus paving the way for the development of each individual according to their needs is what education is all about, then there was no option. Besides, the National Curriculum now requires it.

Taking responsibility

How, though, in practical terms can the work of the languages department be structured to cope with all this? Here are elements of the strategy which is helping us to succeed.

Autonomous learning in each classroom within a department cannot go on simultaneously if the teachers concerned have not among themselves shared the responsibility of preparing materials, deploying resources and working out ways and means for collecting and storing information on pupil progress and achievement. They need to train themselves, negotiate and agree common targets, learn from and support each other. The role of head of department as team leader and mentor is crucial here, as is the understanding that a common approach and philosophy does not mean sterility and uniformity.

Team work

The step from teacher-directed classwork to independent learning is a considerable one and it is important that all concerned understand that the shift in balance of relationships is not an abandonment of responsibility but a way to a greater involvement of the pupil in the learning process. Colleagues outside the language department, senior management, parents and Governors should be made aware of the direction the work of the department is taking, via in-school meetings, schemes of work, minutes of departmental meetings. But most of all, the pupils themselves must be involved in the creation of the learning conditions and environment. This takes time - lesson time - but it is essential to discuss with classes, to listen to suggestions and to incorporate ideas they put forward in the procedures which all will follow. From the formation of working groups within a class, to the acceptance of responsibility for meeting deadlines, caring for equipment, recording progress - the more learners are involved the more

Talking time

readily they will work to ensure the success of the system which they have shared in setting up. Talking time at the start of a new school year or of a new phase of the work is always a worthwhile investment. If teachers and learners write down what they have agreed, then the evidence is there for all to refer to when necessary.

Tables, tasks, tape recorders and tippex

To have ideas is fine, and to negotiate targets and plan procedures gives shape to ideas, but without basic organisation of furniture, books and other resources the theory and good intentions remain just that. The physical proportions of teaching rooms and the arrangement of tables and chairs to allow for small group, pair or whole class work are important in themselves, but imaginative use of floorspace, shelving and movable blackboards can give the kind of flexibility needed. Caretakers and cleaning staff used to years of formal classroom layouts become less hostile to new arrangements if teachers and learners take their full share in arranging furniture and in ensuring tidiness of rooms. If learners are to have open access to books, cassettes, computer, tape recorders, display material and other resources, two elements are essential to the smooth running of operations. Trust has to be built up so that the learners can be given the freedom of access which will allow them to develop independent ways of working. The resources to which they will refer must be organised in such a way that they are easy to find. Colour-coding of topic area tasks, catalogues and lists of books and other resources under topic area (or other) headings, and portable 'kits' - cassette player + junction box + headsets, all help towards a manageable system.

No system or set of procedures can be put in place overnight, but experience has shown that it is better to make a start and to extend, review and revamp than to wait until you have developed a 'perfect' version before taking the plunge. Involvement of the learners at every stage will not only give them a stake in the process but, particularly in the day-to-day organisation and in the assembling and recording of achievement and progress, will show what features of the work they themselves consider important and of value.

Autonomy in the language learning classroom brings freedom and responsibility and in centring attention on the needs of each individual learner will enable us to address more confidently - and more successfully - than before the issues of differentiation and progression.

Jane Hegedus
Cornelius
Vermuyden School,
Canvey Island

Two years ago I arrived as a new HoD at my present school in a department where the staple diet was *Tricolore* and *Deutsch Heute*. I had left a school where four skills group work had long since been introduced and had proved very successful - different groups working on different tasks over a set number of lessons, where pupils were responsible for much of the management of the lesson, setting up and returning equipment, marking completed tasks and monitoring their own assessment.

Trying to get my new department converted was to be a slow process, but gradually we locked away the coursebooks and began to produce our own 'in-house' materials for the four skills group work situation within lower school. Both pupils and teachers adapted well to this change. Pupils no longer waited for the teacher to start the lesson. They knew where to find materials, which tasks they were on, what they had to do next - in fact the lesson could go on without the teacher! Each time a new topic was started, pupils were asked to define their own vocabulary list, discussing in groups which words and phrases they thought they needed to know in order to be able to cope in the chosen topic area.

Pupils were responding well to this way of working. Each seemed to find their own pace and more able pupils were in a position to help the less able in their group. Work was going on with no, or very few, interruptions. I found this way of working quite exciting - different groups working on different tasks. The next step for me seemed quite logical.

I began to produce topic packs of graded activity cards over the four skill areas. After some presentation of initial vocabulary, pupils worked out targets of what tasks they would do over a specified number of lessons (usually 2 x 70 minutes). They could choose to do the tasks in any order they wanted and could decide whether to work as a pair, group or individually. This has worked particularly well in Upper School.

After the Dyffryn conference I felt I wanted to go one step further. I had a year 9 group (more able pupils) of thirty. They had been studying French for two years and had begun German as the second foreign language in year 9, with 3 x 35 minutes French and 3 x 35 minutes German per week.

At the beginning of term 3 they began work on Level 1 German of the Essex GOML scheme. First of all, the class was given the topics. I then gave the group information about where they might find useful and relevant material and set out a list of tasks which needed to be done for each topic:

- prepare and learn a vocabulary list;
- produce and record two role-plays;
- produce a piece of written work, e.g. a menu, cartoon strip, letter, plan of town, etc.

I did set some small assessment tests during this time for my own peace of mind - I needn't have worried.

Pupils researched the topics in pairs or groups. All the old coursebooks and IT packages, once redundant, now had a new lease of life and relevant listening material was provided.

This experiment seemed to be working so well that it was decided to do the work for Level 2 French topics in the same way.

The results have been overwhelming. Pupils have learnt many more structures and much more vocabulary over all the topics than I would have or could have given them in the time they had. All the pupils gained Level 1 German and Level 2 French certificates. I was able to compare their results with other groups and although there was no significant difference either way in the marks obtained, this group had obviously acquired far more than just basic vocabulary.

Most of this group have gone on to study two foreign languages in Upper School. I now intend to try this out with lower ability groups in year 9 and to extend down into year 8.

Steven Fawkes
Beaumont
Comprehensive
School,
Durham

Making resources accessible

Steven Fawkes introduced the idea of the diary or journal which is a key tool in independent learning. This is how he started.

Leni Dam's notion of using a pupil diary as an instrument to record work done, ideas, opinions and plans, was the basis for producing the 'journal' which was tried out by students approaching their GCSE examinations in French. Following mock examinations in December it was clear that different members of the two classes involved had very different needs in terms of practice required and of topics to be revised (or covered at all, in some cases), and there seemed to be little point in teaching the same topic to the whole of the class at the same time through the same means. The experience of the Lane End CILT conference gave encouragement to try to handle this important but difficult phase in a different way.

At the same time it was clear that many of the resources kept in the classroom were being underused and that some items had been given, as far as teachers and learners were concerned, premature retirement.

The first step towards decentralising the working practices of the classroom was consequently to open up the classroom resources to make them accessible to all, whenever they might be needed.

Using the *Journal de travail*

★ Personalise it.

★ Write on front cover principal objectives for the period of the diary (e.g. develop vocabulary in '...' [topic], improve skills in writing letters, etc). Discuss with partners (referring to mock profile sheet) what these objectives should be.

★ Use boxes to: a) record work on speaking, listening, reading, writing, vocabulary and grammar done in class and at home;
              b) highlight (another colour?) work needed and then mark when accomplished.
Work to be marked or checked by teacher should be indicated.

★ At some point each week show your diary to your teacher and discuss where to find materials and how to practice.

★ Use *il faut* box to mark one main objective for next week.

★ If you are getting through a lot of work you may wish to make a larger version of the diary.

★ Use the list of GCSE topics on the back page to steer you to areas you need to study in particular.

This stage included:

1. Making (and publishing) a catalogue of the books stored in cupboards and lockers around the classroom. This was put on the classroom notice board and passed around among colleagues. It was interesting that some books consigned by teachers to a not always respectful oblivion still had attractions for some of the learners. This catalogue was basically a list of book titles with a brief description of the resource, and a reference to where it was to be found.

2. Preparing a borrowing and using system for these materials. A simple check-out and check-in list operated by individual students proved to be workable and to give a reliable idea of where things were.

3. The most time-consuming background work was in compiling a database audit of the materials available for use in class or at home. For this, the Archimedes database *Supastore* was used. A typical record would contain information as follows:

   title of resource
   nature of resource: book/cassette/worksheet/etc
   page reference
   topic covered
   language skills involved
   level: basic/higher

   Learners could then interrogate the database by asking, for example, for a listening activity on the topic of 'eating out'. They could then get a printout of all the relevant activities within all of the resources available.

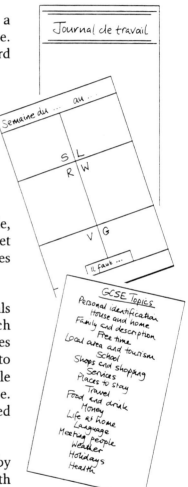

4. In order to make some of the items easier to handle, support materials were created. For example, popular cassette-recorded items which proved to be in demand were re-recorded onto much shorter cassettes in order to make their use more flexible. Similarly, answer sheets to listening and reading activities were made in order to encourage people to check their own work and hopefully re-evaluate their performance. Individual task sheets and vocabulary testing sheets could be requested as and when people completed the topic.

5. A register was put together to operate alongside the journal whereby individuals or groups would request that a certain topic be dealt with in a subsequent lesson, that a certain resource be prepared for their use, or to indicate that a piece of work was ready for marking.

6. The journal itself was prepared and published.

The operation of the journal began with the students agreeing to use it. They spent time initially discussing amongst themselves and with the whole class their performance in the recent mock examinations in the four skills areas, and identifying topics within the GCSE syllabus which they felt needed more attention. They discussed and accepted the following principles for using the journal:

Operation of the journal

- that it was to record all the work they did in French in class and at home in the relevant box - listening work, reading work, speaking work, writing work, vocabulary learning work and grammar work (for those interested);

- that it must be available for discussion in class at all times;

- that it must be trustworthy;

- that all skill areas would need some attention each week;

- that there would be no need to wait for directions at the start of a lesson.

The front page of the journal was for the student to personalise and to highlight his or her main aims for the period covered by the journal (e.g. half a term); this might be development of one particular skill or building up knowledge on a chosen topic etc. The verso of the journal consisted of a list of the relevant GCSE topics to be covered.

Within the journal each page recorded the work of one week in order to give a clear visual clue to which areas were being practised, and which required more work. Similarly, a box was provided for setting a short-term objective for this particular week.

Normally the document would be filled in only by the student although consultation with peers, family and teacher was encouraged and these people could be allowed to record items also. Some people used a different coloured pen to distinguish plans for future sessions from records of what they had done. A further development was made by people bringing into school their own books and resources for use with peers.

At the launch of the journal all save two members of the two classes involved were interested in using it, and at the end of the half-term trial period the students were keen to continue along the same path. At times they requested whole class presentation, and way-stage tests were also established to remind people of the nature of the approaching examinations.

It was pleasing to see people becoming more expert in their selection of materials and activities, and to find them ready to set about their chosen topic for the session as soon as they arrived in the classroom. The straightforward design of the journal and the opening up of the classroom and its resources provided a workable system for both teacher and learners.

Adult and Further Education

In adult education the range of learners, the extent of their previous experience and their expectations can vary widely. Hilary Norris Evans describes her early lessons with faux débutants *while Jan Fornachon recounts her experience with both GCSE and 'A' level learners in the difficult circumstances adult and further education often present.*

Hilary Norris Evans
City of Bath College

GCSE French in one year

Students: false beginners and ex-evening class students; adults of all ages from eighteen to fifty-five in a college of further education.

Aims of students: GCSE/learning French to live in France/learning French for fun.

Two hours a week in class plus as much as they want to do at home.

Lesson 1: students arrive; I ask them to mill around and introduce themselves to each other, in French if possible. Not all students choose to do this. I respect their right to remain silent and to just listen if they want to. Then I introduce myself and my family, with pictures, in French and all have a second go at introducing themselves to their neighbour. Some choose to work in pairs, others in threes. I talk in English about the syllabus, the lack of time, and how much work they will have to do on their own outside class times to pass the examination. Every student who wants to buys a copy of the syllabus and some decide they will stay in the class, but not to do GCSE. I tell them they don't have to make a decision yet, try to de-mystify the syllabus and tell them they can choose how to do it. Some ask for suggestions from me. They are then given a choice of listening comprehension in the language learned. Some do one exercise and then come out and ask to practise introducing themselves again with me; some stay till the end of the class. I offer to make personal recordings for any student who wishes to bring in cassettes they have bought themselves. They have a reference grammar but no textbooks. In retrospect I think they would have liked a textbook to work on at home, but is there a textbook which could be used for one year GCSE?

Materials and activities

For the rest of the year we work as follows: any student visiting France brings back vast quantities of materials for me. I don't even have to collect any material myself, but of course I do. For each lesson or group of lessons I have chosen a topic - sometimes by myself, sometimes by negotiation with the students. They always have a choice of materials and some students manage it all, some a little with my help, and many finish off at home. They give homework to me when they have completed it, never all together - great freedom for them, horrific for me. I try to mark it at home although I should sit down and mark it with them. I think I don't provide enough reading material. Sometimes we watch a video together as a class and then those who want to, watch it again. The quick ones prefer to do extra exercises on grammar or to discuss together. All students often do surveys of the rest of the group which practise points of grammar, vocabulary or functions. They can be as simple as *vous êtes marié/*

célibataire? vous avez un chien/chat/des enfants?, progressing to complicated ones at the end of the year asking about someone's opinions or plans. When they are doing these surveys they have to include me, either to practise on before they ask the others, or at the end of the session when they feel word perfect. Thus I can correct mistakes of pronunciation, grammar, etc without the rest hearing. I also have round-the-class practice, but they ask each other the questions, or I choose a good student to ask the rest. I try not to ask too many questions myself.

Grammar

There is some teaching of grammar. I insist on verbs mainly (to me the backbone of the language): present, future ('going to' only unless they ask for the other), past tense (*Déjeuner du matin* by Jacques Prévert is brilliant for *passé composé*), conditional. I present, then they can do as much practice as they want, mainly from the exercises at the back of their reference grammar or for the stronger ones from *Le grammaire en clair*. They do very little writing in class. It is mainly oral/aural work and quite a lot of text reading. I hate comprehension questions but they seem to like making up really difficult ones to catch each other out.

In one year it isn't possible to cover all the topics so we choose together the ones we like and some of them do the others at home. We start practice for the examinations only after Easter, that is, we stop learning French and learn how to pass the examination. The results last year were that out of sixteen pupils, four chose not to sit the exam but will attempt it next year, eight sat the exam: five got C, one B and two D. We have since decided that we need two years for GCSE.

Jan Fornachon
Barton Peveril College, Eastleigh

My first efforts were a matter of Hobson's choice - an adult flexi-study GCSE French course which my institute had wanted me to run. We had only one scheduled meeting a month and one or two drop-in sessions a month, too. Organisation was of the essence. It was agonising but vital and a supreme example of self-discipline to have to plan a month's work at a time, co-ordinating listening, speaking, reading and writing activities from a variety of sources since no one commercial course (at that time) did a good enough job on all fronts in an acceptable format for adults. I issued packs by post and encouraged students to get together where possible in-between our meetings. Benefits were that the high flyers could work at their own speed, being motivated anyway, but I was surprised by the numbers of those who needed constant teacher input and reassurance, and for whom the course ultimately proved unsuitable. This type of course is, admittedly, an extreme example but later experience with a group of 16+ GCSE retake students showed me how vital it is to be specific about what you are attempting and about expectations from both sides. Full of evangelising spirit from the Lane End conference I shall never forget one lad, who ultimately went on to get a B grade, asking innocently if I would be 'doing any proper teaching' during the rest of the course. I sometimes obliged, normally on major grammar points that everyone needed practice in. This tended to be after problems had arisen - a sort of clinic approach which works well with my 'A' level students: if somebody wants to use an imperative in a piece of oral or written work and can't, that's when we study it. The subjunctive readily enters into its own when the study of man's and the planet's survival is under review: '*il faut que...*', '*j'ai peur que...*' etc.

Organising the materials for the GCSE retake class was a constant battle. I always seemed to be one step behind on answer sheets for comprehension passages in reading and listening, but the appeal of listening on a *Walkman* seemed endless. I kept a file of answer sheets and every student had a record sheet for each unit we covered, to monitor work done and problems encountered.

Motivation is vital in student-centred learning and I am sure validity of tasks plays a vital role here. The perennial penfriend situation, beloved of the examination boards, wears rather thin and I think we need to provide realistic and appropriate tasks for our students wherever possible.

Let them share the responsibilities, too. For 'A' level students let **them** scour *Radio Times* to see what French films might be worth recording. Let one student a week take responsibility for recording the French news and maybe developing simple questions on it or asking fellow students to identify given items of vocabulary. Let **them** bring in items relating to Europe and the language you are teaching from the press. When building up resource banks, try to provide varied material and let students have some choice in the material they use. Should student access material be graded for difficulty? Give **them** a chance to evaluate how difficult they found a given material to use, how motivating they found it. Use techniques from other disciplines - increasingly students are combining non-traditional subjects - take advantage of your mathematicians/ economists, your geographers, historians and artists. Use problem-solving techniques as a stimulus for oral and written work, e.g. installation of a nuclear power station in your area, how to sell your region and boost its economy, designing a leisure park, etc.

Above all, be aware of the language potential in all sorts of situations but don't try to exploit it all/now/all at once. Be prepared to take risks, but you must know what you are trying to achieve and how.

Higher Education

Hilary Norris Evans describes a Higher Education project she was involved in.

Hilary Norris Evans
*City of Bath
College*

I was asked to write all the material for a new course being set up in my college - the Higher Diploma in Administrative Procedures - which combined the business communications and administration with language work for those students who chose that option.

The course was written round an imaginary language consultancy in Chippenham so the students and teachers were put into a working situation, rather than teacher/student relationship. The course ran along supported self-study lines. There was an induction period during which the teachers (it was team teaching) explained how the system would work, elicited student opinion and shared fears and feelings. The students were all to evaluate and monitor their teachers throughout the course. This meant that we really had to think about the purpose and purposefulness of what we and they were doing. Students worked through the assignments at their own speed and in their own way, although they were initiated by the teacher and there was a framework - the assignments we had written and the problem of how to fit them all in. Just like real work. The base room was set up as in business with a meeting area and individual work stations with computers plus a bank of resources which the students were responsible for filing and keeping in order. As well as the mock assignments which we had written, there were many real commissioned ones as well.

An amusing incident to do with autonomy. A meeting had been agreed on to establish a checklist and framework for a new assignment, and various students had promised to inform the meeting about particular issues relevant to the assignment. The meeting started with the teacher sitting next to the Chair and it transpired that no-one had done any preparation at all. All eyes turned to me - after all, I was the teacher, I would save them. I swallowed hard and said that **they** had a problem and they eventually agreed together to fix another meeting when everyone promised to come prepared. A valuable lesson in autonomy for learner and teacher. A colleague who has taken over from me since I left that college remarked: 'All I do is mark and observe, I don't teach any more!'. That's the negative way of looking at autonomy; I prefer the positive way - I learnt with and engaged with the students.

Anny King and Andrew Honeybone
Hatfield Polytechnic

Why the pilot project?

Anny King and Andrew Honeybone (Hatfield Polytechnic) describe their first year of a project which for them and their students was something completely different.

In September 1990 a pilot project in French started within the first year of the BSc Environmental Studies degree at Hatfield Polytechnic. This project aimed to:

- provide a coherent introduction to the study of environmental issues in France;
- use French as the main learning language;
- provide the framework for autonomous language learning.

European integration is a challenging reality. This reality has meant that most programmes of study in higher education now incorporate a language component within their degree. The BSc Environmental Studies degree at Hatfield Polytechnic has an increasing European orientation and thus provides students with the opportunity of taking language courses as part of their programme of study.

Furthermore, these courses can enable students to undertake a sandwich placement with an environmental organisation in Europe during their third year or to participate in exchanges under the Polytechnic's ERASMUS funded ENVIROLINK network involving eight institutions in five EC countries.

But initial experience showed clearly that even the best students gave the language courses lower priority than the rest of their study programme, largely because the language course offered made little provision for their environmental interests and consequently students perceived it as an adjunct to and not an integral part of their course.

Therefore, it was decided to establish a pilot project for first year students which would:

- on the **content** side develop links and coherence between the general environmental course and the French one;
- on the **methodology** side encourage a more independent style of learning.

Introduction à l'Environnement de la France was designed for students with at least a good GCSE standard of French and it was closely related to the environmental content of the other first year courses. After an initial introduction to the geography of France, the French course took some of the environmental topics covered elsewhere in the first year and applied them to specific situations in France. For example, issues such as the role of environmental groups, the use of nuclear power and the development of EC environmental policy were covered. This environmental content was used as the main vehicle for structured language learning.

The combination of environmental content with the development of a more independent style of learning was seen as the principal means of sustaining students' interest and motivation.

To encourage this more independent style of learning, students were encouraged to keep logbooks, not just for recording their progress but also as a means of regular self-evaluation and identification of their own way forward. In addition, emphasis was placed on the development of multi-media dossiers and how to access them. Seminars were held which were designed to develop the students' skills in obtaining information relevant to their needs from videos, audio cassettes and written material.

The course included group, pair and individual work either in class or in the laboratory. The students were timetabled for two hours a week in the classroom plus one hour in the language laboratory. In order to consolidate students' learning and provide them with the encouragement of a demonstrable 'great leap forward', intensive periods of study were included in the course. There was a two-day intensive course at the end of the first semester and a one-week field course in Nord-Pas de Calais at Easter. In both cases, within a pre-determined framework, students were given the opportunity to undertake a variety of tasks which gave them practice in oral and written communication. The intensive course included role-play exercises in preparation for the field course. On the field course itself, in addition to discussions with local environmental experts, the students carried out a questionnaire survey on people's attitudes to the Channel Tunnel. Workshops led by the students and involving about twenty primary school children were the high point of the field course. Preparing for these workshops suggested that rather than make a presentation to the children followed by the usual question time, it might be better for all involved if they discussed environmental issues with small

How did we go about it?

Content of the course

Methodology

Structure

groups of children starting with everyday questions and little by little introducing new data (from the known to the unknown). Also it was felt that involving the children in the workshop was vital and the production of a group poster was seen as a good way to do this. It was a great success all round, not just linguistically but perhaps more importantly pedagogically.

Staffing

In order to improve and consolidate the integration of the environmental content with language learning, a team approach to teaching was adopted. Both language and environmental staff were involved with the planning and the delivery of the course. The environmental staff had a dual role. Whilst they were able to contribute environmental expertise, in terms of language learning they were also students and this provided a useful means of breaking down the barriers between the teacher and the learner and, at its most successful, went further by shifting the emphasis from teaching to learning.

What were the problems?

For both staff and students the environmental French course was a new venture and on reflection we all learnt a lot. However, the difficulty of the enterprise was perhaps not fully appreciated and the initial aims were rather ambitious.

Where did we score highly?

On the negative side we must say that students did not fully understand the importance of logbook keeping and constant self-evaluation. This was partly due to the staff not putting enough emphasis on it and, in particular, insufficient needs analysis meant that the different levels of students' competence were not tackled in a sufficiently systematic way through appropriate teaching and learning styles.

The team also ran into organisational problems due to lack of regular communication between all the team members. Also, the individual roles of staff were not clearly enough defined.

Although seminars on how to access multi-media resources were held, not enough use was made of the facilities provided, due partly to the physical location of the resources and partly to the students not grasping the importance of such a facility. Also, much of the material was being assembled during the year rather than in advance and this hindered some aspects of student preparation. Nevertheless, the collection of environmental material in the multi-media dossiers has provided a valuable resource which though under-utilised in the first year of the project will be of great use in subsequent years.

On the positive side we can say that all students made great strides in understanding, speaking and reading the language at different levels related to their initial ability.

Also, the wide variety of materials which the students handled and the specific tasks they had to perform resulted in their research, organisational and presentation skills being greatly enhanced. Furthermore, the encouragement of a more independent style of learning developed their ability to make decisions and to work in groups with other learners.

The intensive course in the middle of the year and particularly the field trip in the Nord-Pas de Calais were highly successful because within a given framework the students were able either to choose or negotiate the activity they preferred, decide on the style of working and presentation and carry those decisions through. In other words, they were fully engaged in organising their own learning.

Building on the experience gained during the first year, we recognise that there is a vital need to clarify the concept of a more independent learning style. To this end, more attention will be paid to the identification of personal learning plans, individual logbooks and support groups. The use of personal learning plans is seen as a key element of the course, as the plans will be used by individual students to:

What next?

a) clarify their present position;
b) identify their language objectives;
c) find the best ways of achieving these objectives;
d) evaluate their level of achievement.

Following a needs analysis, including a diagnostic test, the logbooks will be used by students to record initial statements on points a) to d) above and then to monitor their progress in achieving their personal objectives. Support groups will facilitate this, working to the mutual benefit of individual students and the group as a whole.

These support groups will also provide a better means of meeting the differing requirements of students with varying initial levels of French language competence. Some will have only a basic GCSE standard whereas others will be of 'A' level standard or beyond. At some points the groups will provide the more advanced students with the opportunity of sharing their learning with their less advanced colleagues. At other times groups will enable students of similar competence to practise their language skills without being overshadowed by their more fluent fellows.

If we are successful in clarifying the notion of a more independent approach to learning, then students will wish to make more use of the multi-media dossiers and other resource materials which have been assembled. Therefore, to encourage self-access to the materials provided, a subject-indexed learner's resources list will be made available to all students and the materials themselves will be made more easily available in the Environmental Sciences Open Learning Centre.

In recognition of the difficulty of adopting a different learning approach in just one element of a degree programme, we would argue that the attempt must be made to adopt a consistent approach across the programme as a whole so that students (and staff) are quite clear as to what is being expected of them. Consequently, more attention will be given to the two-way flow of information and ideas between the French course staff team and other Environmental Studies teaching staff.

To conclude

Chapter 3

THIS IS WHAT HAPPENED: TWO CASE STUDIES

This chapter contains more extended accounts of how two schools introduced and developed a change in teaching and learning styles. In the first case it was one teacher on her own who initiated and followed up the change with the classes she happened to be teaching. In the other it was a departmental decision which was carried through as coherent policy for the teaching of foreign languages throughout the school.

The Boswells Comprehensive School, Chelmsford

Boswells is a 11-18, eight form entry comprehensive school with over 1300 on roll, including 220 in the sixth form. It serves a socially mixed area. The school has diversified its foreign language provision. Half the first year do French, the other half do German and in year 8 half the total start Spanish. Christiane Montlibert is second in a department of nine and has been at the school since 1988.

Christiane Montlibert writes:

Why I started

I arrived at Boswells in September 1988 and amongst my classes I had a top set of second years for French. That year we started doing a lot of group and pair work as they were a lively class, slightly restless but liked to feel involved, organising their role-plays, making dialogues, performing to the rest of the class, putting their hands up, etc.

How I started

Gradually, I asked them to devise their own tasks either in class or at home and they produced excellent work on information-gap exercises for speaking, reading and writing. In those days we were using the old version of *Hexagone II* and we needed to supplement the textbook as it did not lend itself to much pupil-centred learning. So we started carousels which were skill-based using a lot of pupil-designed activities.

Starting carousels

At first, we started a carousel with only two activities: half the class would concentrate on oral pair or group work whilst the other half would do a reading comprehension (or devise one on authentic material) and then swap. I found that group work motivated them because they said it made them feel more secure, it was varied, it matched their potential (was differentiated), and it was a challenge (unexpected format, new elements) although they found they usually succeeded in answering correctly - which boosted their confidence. After these mini-carousels, we launched into four/five skills at the same time (listening, reading, speaking, writing and board-games or computer activities). They carried on with this approach in their third year with a different teacher and also had a go at writing some poetry (see poetry project, page 35).

When they reached their fourth year (we then started calling them year 10) we decided to work on a carousel basis only; we were using *Visa 1* and we also needed a lot of supplementary materials. Our department has a variety of textbooks, sometimes just five copies or so, and we spent part of an INSET departmental day on cataloguing our resources and listing which topics they covered; this exercise helped me devise topic-based learning programmes. I made an arbitrary choice of which topics to treat as we had to fit in with the yearly exams and we followed the contents of *Visa 1*.

Programmes of study

First of all, before starting the linguistic input, we discussed why we should learn such a topic (i.e. house/at home) and already by this stage pupils stated reasons that corresponded to future tasks (i.e. to talk/write about your family and house, to listen/read/talk about other people's, to go house-hunting, to understand property ads, etc).

Then, if it was a brand new topic, I would introduce the new vocabulary and structures myself in the normal way: visuals, repetitions, question/answer oral work, and finally write it all down with a learning and written/reading practice for homework. If it involved revision of vocabulary already studied, I asked learners to make lists of what they remembered and write them out in pairs or groups, allocating house-points to the longest and most accurate lists. Then they would come to the board and write them out for the rest of the class, asking for additions.

At times, I felt that learners would benefit more by doing their own research, accessing textbooks themselves for structures they would hear on tape anyway later during their listening practice and, as they liked copying (they still consider it 'real' work), they had to choose what would be useful to note down from the textbook. I found I had to be quite careful otherwise they would have copied the whole book! So we decided on a time and quantity limit (i.e. no longer than fifteen minutes and no more than twenty structures).

When the research/presentation/revision of vocabulary or structures was over, it was time to start on the practice of different skills using different activities from individual cards or textbooks.

Usually each group decided what activity they wanted to do - sometimes diplomacy and persuasion needed to be used if they all wanted to do the same task at the same time. The basis of their work was collaborative. At times, it meant that some learners would work individually and check their findings with the rest of the group. Usually most of them preferred consulting each other on every point and would only have needed one

Group work

script. In this class, the groups are friendship-based hence they reflect mixed abilities. Pupils worked on their own for homework as well as during formal tests (vocabulary/verb tests, unit tests, essay writing, etc). Each group tended to work at a different pace and the ones who had finished first would usually be given the responsibility of being the 'teachers' and mark others' tasks or help slower learners, once their own work had been marked. Otherwise they could choose to get on with something else ranging from making materials (games, information gaps, reading comprehensions, tests, etc) to reading for pleasure.

Diaries   We all had good feedback of what had been done as each learner had to write a journal, in French, of what had been covered as well as of test marks and impressions on the easiness/difficulty, enjoyment/boredom, or usefulness of an activity or topic (see examples of diaries below).

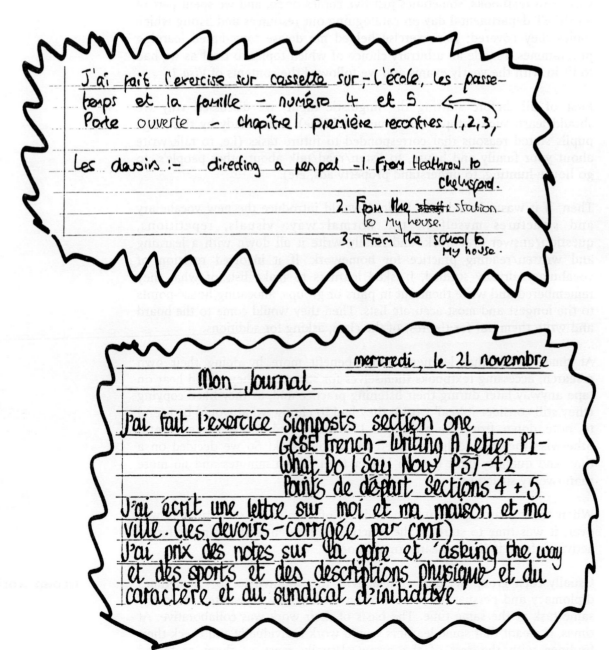

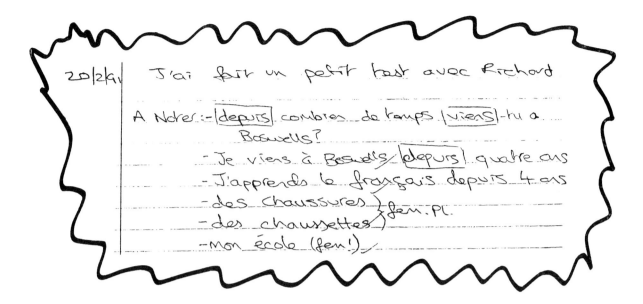

Equipment

All the equipment used was given out by the pupils themselves and put away at the end of a lesson; it meant learning to respect equipment but also to share it, whilst taking a more involved role in the classroom.

We were lucky as we were always in the same classroom, which is set out in six islands of three tables accommodating up to eight learners per group; the floor is carpeted and there are nine power points, two whiteboards, an OHP, a computer (Archimedes), two cassette players and a TV-video.

Preparation for the carousel session would entail monitors giving out textbooks, activity cards, cassettes, junction-boxes and headphones and cassette players as well as making paper available (as they chose to have a file rather than an exercise book). People did not physically move when changing activities, they preferred to move the equipment around (except for the computer). At the end the same monitors would gather all the materials and put them away; these monitors changed every unit and were rewarded with house-points.

'Controlled' autonomy

This way of teaching is not completely autonomous as I never envisaged that each individual would start with the topic they wanted and do whatever task they wanted whenever they wanted. I have devised pupil-centred materials (cutting up old textbooks which I have then mounted on cards and laminated) where learners choose their topics and tasks, but these are for revision/consolidation. As far as new topics are concerned, I still want the whole class to be within the same contextual framework because it helps me to be more organised and keep an easier and more accurate record of their progress.

Motivation

How to get the learners involved? They must feel part of the teaching/learning process: they must talk, ask questions, give answers, express their impressions and feelings and give ideas as far as possible in the target language - but also in English otherwise dialogue might not take place except on purely transactional matters.

GCSE topics

Even when it is teacher's input time, the presentation should start as a problem-solving exercise in the form of whole class or group discussion. For example, the topic on 'complaining' could start with finding out where we might complain, when, what about and how. If done in the target language, a lot of language is already used and can be directly exploited in listening comprehensions or oral role-plays. The role-plays can be designed by the learners themselves; they can make up cartoons and others can change the captions; they can write letters on a specific situation they create themselves or on their own experiences or their parents' (they usually have a wealth of stories to tell!) and of course these letters can be word-processed to look more official and keep up to date with TVEI approaches.

Grammar

Involve learners in grammar by **letting them take the lesson**; the same class, who are now in their 11th year, expressed the burning need to 'go back to tenses'. They felt they had forgotten the present tense, were confused and needed to return to basics. So each group chose a different tense and spent two one-hour lessons and two homeworks preparing a presentation on how to form the tense, the exceptions, examples and practice exercises. They did not need much guidance on their lesson plan and asked for very little help: they asked to borrow textbooks and grammar books and used the relevant chapters or sections to make notes and get ideas for their exercises. They wrote their main points on OHP transparencies (I had an old roll that they cut up in strips) and they asked to have two OHP pens of different colours to highlight endings. The only constraint I put on them was to write a poem in the tense they were presenting to illustrate it creatively and use it as the basis of an information-gap exercise (see poems illustrating tenses on page 38). One group decided to make their presentation in French and therefore revised their commands in the *vous* and *tu* forms.

Without much consultation, they all adopted the same lesson plan. They explained the formation, the endings, gave the exceptions and involved their peers in participating orally. Then they all used different formats of practice exercises ranging from info-gaps, crosswords, word-searches, role-plays, matching up, straight traditional translations, writing a story on a specific theme, to describing a picture.

The 'teachers' imposed themselves firmly and only lost control when they did not give enough time to finish a task or assumed previous knowledge and did not explain a point in detail. For example, one group said: 'the perfect tense with *avoir*, you take the verb *avoir* and you add the past participle; verbs ending in -*er* are easy, you take the r off and put an accent on the *e* = *é*. And now the irregular past participles ...'. At this stage, we had an uproar of people saying they wanted to write all this down and do some exercises on regular verbs and check they could do that before seeing the rest. So they did. The 'teachers' often mimicked my mannerisms without being aware of it as they used the OHP (I tend to point at the board and not the transparency) and encouraged their peers to give answers using encouraging language: *alors, vite, c'est bien, super, excellent, encore, plus fort, je ne suis pas d'accord,* etc. They also organised homework and tests. I was away on a course once and they carried on with the cover teacher who found he did not have to interfere as pupils continued as normal.

The whole project took six class hours - one hour per tense: present, future, perfect with *avoir*, perfect with *être*, imperfect and finally conditional. There were also formal and informal tests as well as corrections of other homework such as listening and reading comprehensions as we felt we also had to practise other skills. This amounted to nine hours, that is, three weeks work. We had an evaluation assessing the whole process. One group prepared the questionnaire on an OHP transparency and chose to follow our departmental REACH interview headings:

Lessons on tenses by 11A 2a

1. Did you find it useful and why?
2. What did you like best?
3. What did you like least?
4. What are your strengths for tenses?
5. What are your weaknesses for tenses?
6. How did it feel being the teachers?
7. What have you learnt?
8. What are your targets? Strategies?
9. Any questions or comments?

Pupils 'in charge'

Most of the answers were very positive as they liked 'being in charge', understood better as 'they were doing all of it', liked 'seeing what it was like to be the teacher' (but did not want to become one!), found on the whole they were less confused over their tenses but needed practice especially in sentence making, found they felt a bit nervous when it was their turn, and felt on the spot when difficult questions were asked. Most of the weaknesses focused on a different tense - especially the conditional as it was new - than the one they had presented (which was their strength) and their targets were to revise and learn the irregular verbs by heart. Under comments, some said they had really enjoyed it but were quite happy for me to return as it was a lot of hard work!

The only incident was that, during the first lesson, Barry (a newcomer to the group) threw a ball of screwed-up paper at David, one of the 'teachers', who is a character well-known for his jokes and his casual attitude to school work. However, on that day David played his role very sensibly and only made a few expected and welcomed humorous remarks. When I analysed the situation with Barry he said he 'could not help it as the lesson was different and not taken by' me. After a short discussion, he agreed that he had been silly and immature and behaved far more responsibly afterwards.

Assessment

Assessment is a very complex issue as the whole educational context is changing and no real document has been produced to be used as a helpful guideline.

A lot of the assessment I carry out with my classes is peer assessment.

- Role-plays are performed to the whole class whose brief it is to give two marks: one for the linguistic content and one for presentation, acting, tone and gestures. This leads to a discussion and negotiation of the final mark.

- A lot of vocabulary tests follow the format of 'write down ten words/structures (depending on age range and ability) on the topic of ... (house, family, station, environment, etc)'. The partner checks in the textbook or exercise book or dictionary and allocates a mark. We have universally agreed to one point per answer (up to three words) and two points per sentence with one/two points off for a misspelling and one point off for a verbal mistake.

- *Tricolore* tests tend to be multiple-choice answers so it is quite easy for pupils to mark each other.

- Obviously some skills are more difficult to assess than others: reading and listening comprehension answers tend to be right or wrong usually because the replies are in English, whereas speaking and writing are based on the production of the target language and involve levels of proficiency. Moreover, several ways of saying/writing something can be correct (*Comment t'appelles-tu? Comment tu t'appelles? Tu t'appelles comment?*) and might not correspond to expected responses. An excellent way of assessing writing without the teacher is to use IT programmes such as *Fun with texts* and let pupils type texts in from a book or from a piece of work already corrected and have others rewrite them filling the gaps, noting their score given at the end by the computer.

- I tend to assess written work myself, but after pupils have had a chance to say where they think they have made a mistake and why. I also give partners a chance to assess each other's writing before I take it in. I think assessment must be seen as part of the learning process. It teaches learners to concentrate and develop the skill of seeing what is right by looking things up and discussing their work with a friend or the teacher.

- It also allows pupils' judgement to be valued by the teacher who is no longer the only one with the Supreme Knowledge; assessing means recognising strengths and weaknesses and acting upon them in order to improve by setting targets for oneself.

- I prefer group or pair assessment as learners seem to pay more attention as the spirit of competitiveness enters into it even with the less able. They prove to be very harsh towards each other and sometimes need to be reminded to be slightly more tolerant ('you said we had to count it wrong if we could not read it; look, is that an 'e' or an 'a'?' when it seems to me that it is an 'e' without any doubt).

- It teaches them to be precise and value accuracy as well as presentation.

- However much as I would like pupils to use self-assessment far more frequently, I must admit that they are not as honest as I would like them to be and I have been disappointed in the outcome many times; I try to avoid this by making pupils use a different coloured pen for corrections.

- Assessment cannot be dissociated from record keeping and evidence; yet again the use of the diary proves to be compulsory as a tool to check what has been covered and what difficulties were encountered or how an activity was perceived.

- I have also let pupils enter their results into my mark-book themselves so they can get feedback on what they have achieved and how they have performed and progressed over several weeks. Again, it gives them a great sense of responsibility and they react very positively.

More! And encourage other members of the department to adopt this way and get together to make up more materials. Most of my TVEI time this year is spent on producing resources for pupil-centred/flexible learning that we then try out whilst team teaching. Questionnaires are also designed for pupils to express their feelings, for more dialogue and negotiation to take place and to help us improve the tasks.

What next?

Christiane describes three particular projects which she has organised: the Poetry Project, the project on the environment and some sixth form work.

The *National Curriculum Working Group Initial Advice* published in February 1990 mentioned poetry in the Writing Attainment Target. I decided to set up a poetry project with two classes as our participation in the July 1990 East Anglia Festival of Modern Languages.

The Poetry Project

The two classes were second year set 2 and third year set 3 (we have four sets of ability). Both classes had produced collaborative work before but on more traditional topics. Both had their disruptive elements and I used the project to motivate them after their exams had long been finished.

I introduced the project and its purpose as producing a display for the Festival and breaking out of routine and doing something 'completely different'.

*Input
Lesson 1:
one hour*

First we discussed what poetry meant and the different sorts of poems found (in English and very rapidly). Then I gave a few examples of French poems and pupils found that they rhymed at the end, so in class we started looking for words we knew that rhymed.

Homework that day was to find more words that rhymed from the *lexique* part of the textbook and from previous lessons.

The next classwork consisted of sharing our research: pupils wrote their lists on the board and others were added to them. When mistakes in rhyme were made, we discussed them together and corrected them, i.e. *a/est, souvent/mangent, frère/soeur, on/en*, etc. We talked a lot about silent final letters and different sounds, but we also agreed on poetic licence, i.e. *on/en/ant, pas/moi.*

*Acquisition
Lessons 2 and 3:
two hours*

Then we had a go at writing the poem with the whole class participating, using the blackboard/OHP, and individuals adding their variations.

Voilà mon chat
Il s'appelle Nicholas
Il aime le lait
mais il déteste le café

Ma soeur
aime les fleurs
mais elle déteste
le beurre

J'ai un père
une mère
un frère
j'habite dans une maison
et il y a un salon
trois chambres et une salle à manger
et une salle de bain
dans la cuisine il y a du pain

Finally, I asked pupils to work in groups or in pairs, as they wanted, and using their amended lists of rhyming words their task was to write a poem on any theme, of any shape and of any length they wanted. All I did then was to circulate, answer queries, discuss possibilities, sometimes help to start, and correct mistakes explaining why. I found myself doing far more grammar than I expected as they needed structures to link their words and only tended to use infinitives. It gave them a new dimension to using verbs and endings in context.

Choices were unexpected and the end product was a great variety of themes, shapes and levels of language and degree of imagination. It was not at all reflective of the learners' expected abilities: some fast learners were impeded by their lack of imagination and needed a lot of guidelines whilst some less able learners revealed a truly poetic nature and required no reassurance. Some results were totally surprising and brilliant, like Lucy's flower and the *Fusée du futur*.

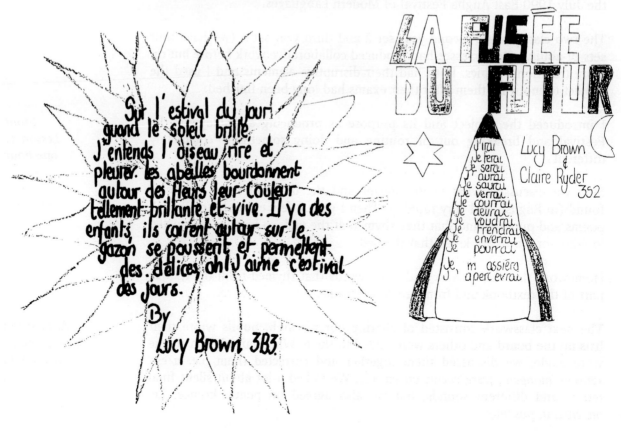

I found pupils totally involved as it was a novelty and non-threatening; they genuinely collaborated and did everything - writing, colouring, cutting, sticking, etc. Many asked to carry on at home and produced twice as much as I had planned.

When the display was completed, they presented their poems to the rest of the class and read them aloud, sometimes giving a loose translation if others did not understand. They also asked each other why they had chosen such a theme and how they had proceeded, which allowed everybody to take part and to express themselves publicly on their own achievements. They were very proud of their work and therefore reacted in a responsible manner to the presentation and discussion.

Consolidation
Lesson 4:
one hour

On 14 July 1990 the poems were exhibited at the East Anglian Festival of Modern Languages at Colchester and won a prize and were sent to represent our school at the National Festival at Warwick University in October 1990.

It provided us with a total change; the emphasis being on sounds and themes and personal flexibility. Pupils were autonomous as they only used me as part of their resources, facilitating the end product. They also made an efficient use of dictionary skills as they looked up linking words. They had no constraints such as 'write a letter about ...' and were able to use their French to create a piece of writing, be it concrete or abstract.

Evaluation

In 1991 I decided to involve my years 11, 12 and 13 in this sort of creative writing and my year 11 used poems to explain tenses to the class; their carousel was for each group to concentrate on one tense and present/explain it to the rest, using role-plays, activities, listening, etc. I only gave one example 'Conjugaison interrogation' by Jean Tardieu from *Formerie* (Gallimard) and after that they hardly needed me; some groups put their poems on OHP transparencies, turning them into cloze exercises or 'find the ending' exercises.

Further
developments

My year 13 worked on *Voyelles* by Rimbaud using the association of ideas concept; once again they did this collaboratively but some wrote their own at home.

Year 9 worked on creative writing on Paris (*Tricolore III*) making a visual display of poems and photos and postcards/drawings.

I have found it a most rewarding experience where the foreign language genuinely met feelings and conveyed them in an original format; I felt impressed by the outcome and the sense of achievement and enjoyment it communicated to learners. It has inspired me to carry on and develop this form of creative writing at every level, for concrete or abstract language. I recommend it as a way of boosting confidence and providing variety in the writing skill. Try it, you won't regret it!

Conclusion

*Poems
illustrating
tenses*

Mes Jours d'enfance

Quand j'étais petit,
J'étais enfant unique
Je m'amusais,
Avec mes jouets je jouais.
La télé je regardais,
"Les Stroumfs" J'adorais.
J'allais chez le Père Noël,
Sa grotte était belle!
Sur la plage je jouais,
Dans la mer je nageais.
Toutes les choses je faisais,
Mes jours d'enfance j'adorais!

Andrew Jauncey
Tim Speakman
Dawn Thrift
Katy Lloyd.

Si j'avais
assez d'argent
J'achèterais
une maison

Si je n'avais
pas assez d'argent
j'achèterais
des gants

Si j'avais
une fille
Je l'appelerais
Camille

Si j'avais
un fils
Je l'appelerais
Maurice

Si j'avais
une mini
je conduirais
à Paris

Si j'avais
un avion
je voyagerais
au Japon

Que feriez-vous?

Caroline
Christie
Laura
Mel
Helen
Rosemary.

Une Semaine

Lundi je suis né,
Mardi j'ai mangé,
Mercredi j'ai ri,
Jeudi j'ai dormi,
Vendredi il a plu,
Samedi j'ai bu,
Dimanche je suis mort.

Barry Malill

Sixth form poem

VOYELLES.

Pour moi A est la chaleur du soleil,
Brillant coeur doré d'une marine moule;
Passion profonde, une seule rose pourpre,
Lance du diable aux trois pointes, cruelle,

Est E. Le soir étoilé enchanté,
Le velours noir, I la troisième voyelle,
Dans l'espace le parfum augmenté,
Des flocons couvrant les montagnes gelées

La candeur est O, couronnant la piste,
Mais U est seulement bleu, l'eau, ciel et triste.

With my year 10 class we also did a project on the environment with Lid King from CILT. It was based on materials used with non-specialist adult learners and aimed at teaching school pupils an environmental topic in the target language (French) studying largely if not exclusively authentic materials for language input, and developing the maximum degree of pupil involvement and independent learning. The materials were the video of *Lessives polluantes* broadcast by Antenne 2 and reshown on Olympus (3 mins), a cassette of the soundtrack of the video, the song by Jean Ferrat called *Restera-t-il un chant d'oiseau*, an advert on pollution from MPG *Thématique*, a brochure on sources of pollution and a game produced by the CILT post-16 course 1990.

Project on the environment

The input was presented by the teacher: pollution and the aim of the project. The class then divided into self-selected groups to work on their brainstorms (what was the expected language?) and after ten minutes their lists were compiled. Then the video was watched without the sound and the groups noted down what they saw or found words that they needed. Finally the song was played and the words distributed. Homework was to complete the linguistic prediction exercise on pollution with a dictionary and to translate the song into English.

The second one-hour lesson focused on acquisition after an initial class check on vocabulary and phrases learnt. The format used was a carousel: video (group watching with sound and prepared lists, identifying heard sounds, checking afterwards with the *texte visuel*); tasks using the video sound track only; sound (cloze text - verbs - of song); written texts (exploitation task on OHP in French from *Thématique*); puzzle (match visual to text). The homework was to devise a puzzle or test and revise the vocabulary/phrases.

The next lesson aimed at consolidation and groups decided what tasks they would display to the rest of the class and brought in pictures to help. They produced:

★ a poster on ecology
★ a poster on pollution
★ a brochure on different aspects of the problem
★ a TV discussion with mother, daughter, ecologist, industrialist
★ a poem/song
★ a radio interview with schoolchildren

The last lesson concentrated on the completion of the tasks and their filmed presentation in French to the whole class. Their homework was to write a newspaper article on the environment.

The conclusions were that it is possible to teach 'real' subjects to groups below the age of sixteen. Interest and the ability to work independently are key factors. Learners know much more linguistically and culturally than we often think. Talking and sorting things out is not wasted time. Independence does not mean no system: they needed games, tests, checks, etc to show that they were making progress. In their evaluation of the project all pupils said they had found it interesting and therefore relevant (see pupils' evaluation below) - except one. Such work does depend on good pupil-pupil and teacher-pupil relationships. These learners can do much more than we ask of them.

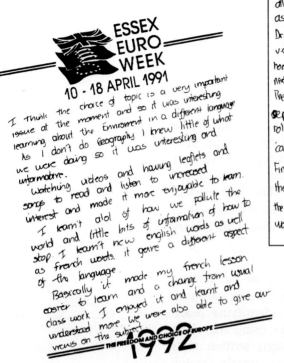

I think the choice of topic is a very important issue at the moment and so it was interesting learning about the Environment in a different language. As I don't do Geography I knew little of what we were doing so it was interesting and informative.

Watching videos and having leaflets and songs to read and listen to increased interest and made it more enjoyable to learn.

I learnt a lot of how we pollute the world and little bits of information of how to stop. I learnt new english words as well as french words. It gave a different aspect of the language.

Basically it made my french lesson easier to learn and a change from usual class work. I enjoyed it and learnt and understood more. We were also able to give our views on the subject.

The project began with an introduction to 'The Environment'. We all wrote down the words in French we already knew that were associated with the environment. All the words were put together and Dr. King gave us some new words or phrases. We then saw a french video about the environment and had to write a script for it. For homework we had to translate some phrases and a song. With the next lesson we listened to some questions on the song and answered them. The song was also translated properly!! The next lesson we began separate things to show what we'd learnt. Some made a role play and some produced a poster. We also finished the 'carousel' topics - for us the proper script for the french video.

Finally we showed our work to the class. The topic of the environment is relevant to everyone and learning the french for the phrases was interesting. French was spoken all the time, so the words and phrases were learnt fully.

Sixth form work

We are doing the AEB board 'A' level examination and we study a region of France as one of the 'Civilisation' topics. We chose the Loire Valley because we have an exchange with the Collège G Brassens in Esvres near Tours for years 9 and 10 and with the Lycée A de Vigny in Loches for years 11, 12 and 13. Over the past we have collected documents, books, bought French geography textbooks; we have written to different *Chambres de Commerce* and *Syndicats d'Initiatives* as well as liaised with the French exchange history, geography and economics teachers to increase our information on the area.

Two years ago, my lower sixths used all this and produced *exposés* - word processed or typed with illustrations, diagrams, graphs, postcards, leaflets, maps, synoptic tables and vocabulary lists - on one chosen aspect of the region. After I marked their work, which they did collaboratively, they edited their copies and produced a five/six page *exposé* which they presented to the rest of the class and also photocopied for their peers. The themes were:

La Vallée de la Loire

La géographie et le climat	*L'histoire*
Les villes principales	*Le patrimoine culturel (châteaux,*
L'agriculture	*gastronomie,traditions et légendes)*
L'industrie	*Les transports*
Le commerce	*Les changements récents et prévus*
Le tourisme	

Since that time, I use these *exposés* as the basis for our study and ask my present students to update or delete the information presented. Again, because learners were at the very centre of the research and learning process, their interest was increased and they retained the major points far better than if they had been lectured to.

Hanham High School, Bristol

The teachers in Hanham High School arrived at a form of independent learning as a way of extending language study to low achievers and especially those with special educational needs (SEN). What they did will appear revolutionary to many teachers but will have very familiar elements for others. The following account shows the way one group of teachers in a fairly typical school argued their way through the demands of a situation to a, for them, completely different teaching and learning style. ISOPS is the acronym for Individual Student Orientated Programmes of Study.

Hanham High School is a six form entry comprehensive school on the eastern outskirts of Bristol. It was opened in 1977. Languages have been taught to all pupils to the age of sixteen from the outset.

Why we set up ISOPS

ISOPS was targeted at the two parallel lower groups in year 9, i.e. groups 9.3. There are no specific remedial classes, so 9.3 groups contain all pupils who are considered by us to fall in the lower third of the ability range. There are no exceptions.

9.3 groups had received what seemed to be a successful course based on the 'South West Credit' graded tests. It was felt that this was stagnating and was dependent largely on 'strong'/experienced staff. It provided a relatively small range of language which deprived the more capable members of the set, which contained one third of the ability range, from progressing further even if it favoured those less able to remember vocabulary. In short, it was not possible to say that we were really addressing the needs of all the pupils in these groups.

The 9.3 groups arrive in their classes very aware of their standing in the pecking order and their self-esteem may be very low. Self-confidence cannot be taken for granted. They contain children who have a host of differing needs. These include emotional needs, learning difficulties and behavioural problems.

It is unfortunate but true that those who perceive that they are failing become very conscious of the quality of what they receive by way of school input and 'investment'.

Challenging assumptions

It is perhaps stating the obvious that any permanently teacher-directed classroom inevitably suffers from a degree of dependency that has always caused modern linguists a good deal of concern. We are forever aware of the problem of being the lone expert. But the didactic system of teaching causes problems for some pupils more than others.

The problems confronting SEN pupils in the whole class situation are not inconsiderable and tend, understandably, to be overlooked by the hard-pressed classroom teacher who is having to teach a group of thirty pupils at a time. At no point would we wish to claim we have imagined that it is possible to address all the difficulties that SEN pupils have to struggle with, but there are certain elements of their misery that can be regarded as suitable cases for treatment.

For instance, the self-image of the SEN pupil suffers considerably from constantly seeing a large number of his/her peers performing better orally, something that for many low achievers is extremely difficult to emulate: speaking a foreign language in public. Only the removal of the fear of public humiliation (and it has been expressed in those sort of terms by some of our low achievers) will begin to address this problem realistically.

It is also difficult for SEN pupils to acquire information in the whole class situation. The relationship with the teacher at the front is a distant one, particularly for those who traditionally feel safest at the back.

There is an irony in that low achievers are clearly the pupils in any class who most need to ask questions. It is hardly surprising that low achievers find it difficult to raise points in public with their teacher. We have to accept that their poor self-image in academic terms is usually not divorced from their social self-image.

Therefore, the very distance that lies between an SEN pupil and the source of information or learning must determine to some degree how easily he or she is able to cope with it. Indeed it is not entirely ridiculous to ask whether a low achiever cannot learn more from a relatively incapable neighbour than a more distant, preoccupied specialist despite the drawbacks. The very fact that pair and group working is now common practice in language learning must surely demonstrate the point. It is therefore more a question of degree than any 'dangerous' theory under consideration here. ISOPS is all about extending such partner and group practice across the board to the advantage of the low achiever.

The assumptions we challenged were as follows:

- that a set is a teachable entity, irrespective of the range of ability, any SEN children it may contain and even pupils who may have difficulties in your particular subject. It is all too easy to view a set as representing a certain level of potential without considering in detail those of whom it is composed.

- that a coursebook caters for the needs of all pupils. After all, is not a coursebook someone else's idea of pupils' needs? It is not written with any particular class in mind.

- that a didactic teaching method caters for all pupils in a given class, and that a working atmosphere is ensured; that the only effective learning comes from the teacher, if indeed it is to be assumed that a large proportion of the pupils learn from didactic teaching to any appreciable degree.

- that traditional patterns of assessment successfully analyse pupil performance. We suggest that they often at best confirm a good teacher's previously formed notions, and often point to strong and weak points of teacher performance without improving the pupil's. In fact, poorly used, they can be a considerable demotivator.

How we went about it

Those assumptions challenged, we had to set about a radical move from the traditional teaching stance. The point of departure with ISOPS is that the teacher is removed from the front of the classroom and joins a battery of resources. The responsibility for pupil's learning shifts to either a small pupil collective or, quite often, the individual pupil him/herself with, we hoped, major advantages for SEN pupils.

Our approach to the whole issue of setting up a new course was determined by two constraints which we are certain affect most classroom teachers:

★ lack of time to meet and discuss developments beforehand;
★ lack of time to produce a completely new range of materials.

We would be the first to accept that there is much to be said for a run-up process of theoretical discussion and planning. But we lacked time. We agreed that we would learn from our mistakes and either improve on our failings or else, if we felt that the whole scheme was proving an undiluted failure and disadvantaging the students, we would have the courage to abandon it before it became a burden to staff and pupil alike.

We decided to base the course around the topics in *Destination France*. The topics immediately created a 'spine' to the organisation of resources which spared us the worry of setting up something entirely different 'just for the sake of it'. Our experience told us that low achievers are quite ready in this day and age to accept that a visit to France is no pipe dream; the transactional language that dominates the course content makes excellent common sense to them.

The chief benefit from our act of pragmatism was that we could begin to develop resources to complement *Destination France*. The pupils regard it as a sheet anchor in their work and would never dream of not consulting it at the outset of any unit, even though there is an array of more demanding and exciting resources around them. The very simplicity of the book appeals to them when they are least sure of what they are doing.

The development of this course alone has vindicated the Faculty's decision some time ago to buy in a word-processor for administration and materials development. The ISOPS course has certainly benefited from our acquired experience in word-processing, not only in terms of written resources but also storage management. Indeed, it would be very doubtful whether we would have undertaken such a project had we not been able to rely on the support of our WCP.

The key change, as we stated at the beginning of this section, was the decision to transform the teacher into a resource. The resources must be varied, not just a selection of worksheets. Variety of media is important. Even more essential is that when the teacher's hands come off, as it were, and he or she relinquishes control of the resources in a classroom situation, then the individual pupil's hands must come on. This meant that pupils would have control of video, computer etc. It was a natural concomitant of the individualisation of a pupil's learning.

How ISOPS works

The essentials for any course unit are:

● An 'I can' sheet. This sheet clearly lays out the objectives for the unit, hopefully in terms that all pupils can understand. All pupils stick this sheet in their books and can make a note when they feel that they have achieved a certain objective.

● A 'Resources sheet'. This sheet details all the resources which are available for a given unit. Again, each pupil has their own copy and can keep a record of what they have used.

● The multi-media resources themselves:

- teacher
- foreign language assistant
- books
- worksheets from a variety of sources
- a classroom computer
- listening centres and cassette recorders
- video programmes

All the above resources can be used through systematic programming or 'one-off' activities. They can also be used to provide differentiation between the activities of pupils with different strengths and weaknesses. In other words, they are all highly adaptable to individual needs. ISOPS provides the framework within which such usage can be managed.

● Assessment materials. The principal aim of these is to encourage as well as test.

● A record of achievement. This is clearly designed to be formative and includes an element of pupil-accepted accountability.

Teaching methods

Traditional methods are restricted to settling the class, clearing up and imparting any new information about resources. All other work is approached on a teacher to group/individual basis. It was intended that the pupil should use resources to achieve the objectives on the 'I can' sheet independently. The teacher acts as a resource and also guides individuals or groups, particularly providing them with opportunities to listen and speak. In this respect it is easier to see to pupils with special needs.

Assessment and records of achievement

There is no doubt in our minds that the nature of testing and grading often pre-determines not the level of success but the level of failure in most students. We highlighted before that assessment merely acts as a quality control device for teaching staff rather than an operation that benefits pupils.

Nonetheless, we had no intention of doing away with testing in the creation of our ISOPS courses. We were quite aware of how important tests and results are to our pupils. But assessment had to avoid confirming their worst fears as they entered the classroom for the first time; they had after all carefully considered the standing of their new-found classmates and were already marking themselves down as a result.

Bearing such a reaction in mind, it is crucial that testing becomes a positive device in the system, something that shows pupils how **well** they are doing, even if it also serves to pinpoint some of the failings at the same time. Both functions have become increasingly integrated into the operation of the course's records of achievement in a very positive fashion.

An essential prerequisite of any testing material is that it can be deemed fair by the pupils. They are armed with an 'I can' style objectives list which serves as a guide to their work. It would be a monumental own goal if our testing material should demand something that is not on that list.

We have even gone as far as stating that certain resources may contain items of information that relate very closely to the forthcoming test material. The pupils see this as an advantage; we see it as a way of encouraging them to use resources that may be less favoured but which are essential to their language development, such as audio tape. We find this a practical measure whilst we try to evolve more stimulating listening materials!

Basically, the assessment materials are as follows:

- Listening test
- Reading test (which includes a small element
   of written production on occasions)
- Speaking test

For the sake of order and fairness, the first two items are conducted as a classroom exam. The speaking test is conducted by the teacher with individuals at the back of the class whilst the other pupils are working. We would not prevent a pupil from taking the exam two or more times if they so wished.

Nonetheless, we have sought to evolve other styles of testing. It has been possible to set up a software programme on the trolley-borne computer which acts as a stimulus: a changeable clock. Two pupils test each other (thus promoting the use of question as well as answer) and the teacher merely sits as an observer.

Pupils are asked to assess for themselves their performance over the recent unit. Ideally, they do this before they receive their test marks. They tend to underestimate their worth and so the test results come as a pleasant surprise. These assessments are kept to a very simple 'Happy' or 'Unhappy' with respect to the following:

- Their opinion of their test performance.

- The usefulness for revision of:

  - video tapes;
  - audio tape notes;
  - general written notes from worksheets etc.

The review of pupils' principal writing work, i.e. their notes, is operated in terms of their usefulness as a learning tool: has the pupil produced notes that are valuable during the process of revision for the test itself?

The self-assessment of presentation and effort is based on the school's own grading of effort, namely:

A = working to best of ability
B = room for improvement
C = cause for concern

It is interesting to note that pupils are often very hard on themselves and the individual discussion with staff is often an opportunity to give encouragement and praise.

Therefore, the whole style of recording achievement is clearly formative. It serves as a focal point for discussion and serves to encourage the individual low achiever to assess strengths and weaknesses, dividing work up into specific areas easily recognised by the pupil because they relate to the activities in the classroom. It is possible to identify specific areas for improvement. The record of achievement sheet allows the teacher to gently guide the pupil to plan improvements.

Records of achievement to the rescue

Records of achievement also solved a major difficulty for us at the outset. We became embroiled in a complex and bureaucratic system to check pupils were managing a variety of resources successfully. We were in danger of becoming over-directive and, moreover, in their inimitable fashion pupils were subverting the system anyway! By requiring them to account for the work on a resource on their record of achievement sheet, we ensured pupils were not too far off course but without reducing their freedom to approach each unit in their own way. As a consequence, individual use of all resources designated by the record of achievement has increased a great deal.

Teacher response

We cannot pretend, looking back, that we had no hesitation in what seemed to be the letting go of traditional control. It did worry us. But we have been impressed by the atmosphere which has grown up in the ISOPS classroom. Standards have been generally high and we feel that expectations for the majority of pupils have been raised.

We have been very encouraged by pupil reaction to the scheme. Motivation has certainly been raised as the question of self-esteem has been addressed. Pupils for the most part enjoy being 'in charge' of their own learning and are prepared to accept responsibility for this when records of achievement are discussed.

Teaching has been just as demanding/tiring but there has been an increase in effective pupil/teacher contact. We have been able to commend pupils for success in the language but also in the management of their learning. We have also been very alive to pupil opinion.

We have learned a great deal of new ways (for us anyway!) of resource and classroom management as a result of this scheme. The very flexibility that ISOPS imparts creates an environment that promotes change and experiment. Whilst we recognise that there are improvements still to be made, we remain in no doubt that ISOPS is a great improvement for our low achievers and is successfully challenging the assumptions which we outlined at the start of this paper.

Chapter 4

WHAT DO I DO AND HOW DO I DO IT?

The first chapter was an attempt at an answer to the question: how do I get started? Once started, you begin to ask yourself a lot more questions. This chapter tries to answer the most common ones, drawing on teacher experience.

What do I do if I only have *Tricolore/Deutsch Heute/etc?*

It depends how adventurous you want to be. The suggestions below, and they are only suggestions, start with tinkering and end with root and branch reappraisal.

1. Within your ordinary style of teaching you can add more independent activities like those mentioned at the beginning of Chapter 2, i.e.:

    - learners choosing the vocabulary words to learn;
    - learners choosing which exercise to do or the order in which they are done;
    - learners choosing to do those parts of an exercise they feel confident about - they should explain their difficulties over the ones they have left out and they should not feel they have to do something they are going to do badly;
    - learners working on exercises in pairs or groups.

2. Have a carousel of activities taken from the book so that not all the class is doing the same thing at the same time. Re-record the sections of the tape onto separate cassettes so that one group can do a listening exercise.

3. Let the class read through the unit themselves and in groups/pairs decide which part they want to do first. They must then work out whether another part of the unit has to be worked through before they can do the part they have chosen. They should be encouraged to work

out what that part of the unit is trying to teach them, and what they know about it already.

This can be recorded in their exercise book or diary, e.g.:

section of unit chosen ...
what it is trying to teach us ...
what we know about it already ...
what we have to do before we can do this unit ...

Eventually, all this recording will be in the foreign language.

4. Put up the title of the next unit.

    a. Say: This is the title of the next unit in the book. Ask: What do you expect it to be about? What is it going to try to teach you? What words do you know about it already? What new words would you expect to meet?

    b. Learners should look right through the unit and make a list of what it is trying to teach them.

    c. Learners add to the list anything else within the topic they would like to learn.

    d. A report back session to the whole class about objectives discovered and proposed. They should perhaps agree at this point that some reading, listening, speaking and writing must be done within the objective.

    e. A discussion of what functions will be required: e.g. will you need to know how to ask questions, how to say what has happened/is going to happen, how to say things are bigger/smaller, etc?

    f. Groups decide which parts of the unit they will start with (see activity 3).

    g. The groups work on the objectives, including deciding what they do for homework.

    h. They decide how they can show they have reached their objective - by completed exercise, creation of role-play, oral report (in the foreign language), etc.

    i. Report back to the whole class of work done in each group with demonstrations where appropriate.

    The idea here is to get learners to realise that the textbook is a tool that they themselves can control in order to make their learning easier.

David Little reports in his book, *Learner autonomy: definitions, issues and problems* (Authentik, 1991), an experiment by Jean-Pol Martin of the University of Eichstätt in Bavaria:

David Little

> *Jean-Pol Martin divided a French class into groups and the groups took turns to teach the rest of the class. In that instance the language course book was chosen by the teacher but the pupils accepted responsibility for the choice by agreeing to use it as the basis for their learning. And of course the group of learners responsible for teaching a particular unit to the rest of the class could not help but make it their own in the way they prepared and communicated it.*

To get a class to teach the whole of the textbook to each other requires nerve by both teacher and taught. It is, however, possible to agree with the class that groups should teach the others, starting with quite small segments - the vocabulary of clothes or parts of the body, how to tell the time, etc.

Christiane Montlibert, whose class groups took turns in teaching tenses to the rest of the class using material from the coursebook (see page 32), writes:

Christiane Montlibert

What do I do if I only have *Tricolore*? First, I discuss why the class is going to do the topic, e.g. *'Prendre le métro à Paris'*. They have a helpsheet for each unit and a menu of activities to be followed, if possible in the target language: *'premièrement lisez comment prendre le métro, puis avec votre groupe faites un dépliant en anglais pour votre école. Ensuite, faites les exercices p9/10 oralement avec votre partenaire. Quand vous aurez fini, faites le quiz au brouillon et préparez un quiz vous-même sur le métro de Paris ou de Londres (en français, bien sur!)'* etc.

Pupils can be responsible for teaching each other and the whole class chooses topics, especially the peripheral topics such as being ill, reporting an accident, complaining, at the lost property office, etc. Each group decides what topic they want to present and looks in all the textbooks, resources, realia, etc the school possesses. If need be get a loan from the nearest (European) Resource Centre or Teachers' Centre. Learners make lists of vocabulary and structures, make role-plays, listening and reading comprehensions, use an OHP and/or a video, prepare situation cards, etc to introduce the topic to their peers or to revise it. It is far more interesting; they are directly involved; they learn better.

The same applies to the teaching/revising of tenses, especially with year 10, 11, 12 and 13 classes.

How do I get the room organised when I occupy it only one period each time?

Train the class to reorganise the furniture and get on with the task in hand as soon as they get into the classroom and without specific orders from you. The occasional timing of this (like a fire drill) helps to keep them on their mettle. Similarly at the end of the lesson. The instructions should be taught as other instructions are (see the question on decoding instructions on page 58).

How do I organise carousels?

Vee Harris

Whatever approach is adopted, things need to be as tightly structured, if not more so, as for a teacher-dominated lesson. This can make for a great deal of extra work for the teacher but one way round it is to involve the pupils in the organisation - everything from moving the furniture, to transporting equipment, to their own assessment. One teacher noted that when she let pupils select the tasks for themselves, they were more motivated and therefore concentrated better. This in turn reduced the noise level, which can be a problem. Have a clear structure to the way you organise things:

- Put the names of the groups out on the tables, so that pupils come in and are immediately seated in groups. Give the groups a name (group A, B, C, etc) so that the teacher can monitor who does what.

- Have the tasks that each group is meant to do, or the menu of possible tasks and their order clearly displayed on a wall-chart or a progress sheet. Have the tasks themselves or the resources in clearly labelled folders, or boxes at the front of the room.

- When one task is finished, the group must tick it off on the wall-chart or the progress sheet so the teacher can keep track of their progress for the next lesson.

- In a carousel model, most of the teachers preferred to let pupils move on when they were ready rather than moving all the groups on at particular points in the lesson. This can, however, cause a log jam (e.g. if one group hasn't finished listening to the tape, the others are kept waiting). You need to have at least one extra activity available which pupils can be doing while they are waiting, or extra copies of the same activity.

In terms of the tasks, these should not be so long that they are not possible to finish in one lesson - pupils should be left with a sense of achievement. They should also end with an open-ended task to allow for early finishers and also for a more creative use of the language.

How do I form groups?

There are many conflicting opinions, no easy answers and there are arguments both for and against most solutions. A group of more able learners, for example, may go faster when together, but mixed ability groups allow less able learners to be supported by the more able who in turn learn more efficiently from having to make their own knowledge explicit. One of the quickest ways to learn is to have to teach. Similarly, learners may feel more secure working with friends but that does not develop their ability to collaborate successfully with a range of people. One of the best rules seems to be that in the course of the year learners should have the opportunity to work with all the other members of the class.

Marian Carty, Advisory Teacher for Modern Languages, Merton, and Vee Harris have used the following devices for organising groups.

Marian Carty &
Vee Harris

- Pupils are given a number from one to four. Then all the 'ones' work together, all the 'two's' and so on. Or they are given cue cards, so that they must find the four other people in the class who like history/have a picture of a particular fruit.

- Through teacher-determined criteria - for example, one more able pupil, one less able, one artistic, one sociable, etc.

- Through a mixture of pupil choice and teacher criteria - for example, teacher chooses group leader, group leader chooses friend, friend chooses someone of the opposite sex.

- Through pupil choice - 'you can work with a friend but then you must choose a pair of friends to work with that you haven't worked with before'.

- Through the nature of the task itself, which may lend itself best to:

  ★ ability groupings according to whether pupils need to practise/consolidate what they know or whether they are ready for extension activities.

  ★ balance of gender/race in groups if an aspect of equal opportunities is to be dealt with in part of the topic covered. Clearly, however, great sensitivity will be needed by the teacher to handle such decisions successfully.

  ★ single-sex groupings in speaking or IT tasks to ensure that boys do not 'take up all the space'.

- Interest groupings. Pupils may have a free choice from a menu of tasks, grouping themselves according to whether they want to do a listening or a reading task, or tackle one aspect of a topic rather than another.

The teacher will need to monitor the groupings and assess their achievement, as a prelude to making decisions about the best way to proceed. The pupils themselves can be invited to take on increasing responsibility and to participate in these decisions. As is the case with whole class interaction, the more pupils are involved in the process, the more likely it is to succeed.

How do I get groups to work collaboratively?

Some groups settle down immediately, others take time to gel, some never seem to. It usually helps to make explicit the reasons for working collaboratively and what is involved. Not all work can or should be done collaboratively but where it is, the purpose is for the group to work as a team. That is, the members should use each other as resources before asking the teacher, should listen carefully to each other, support each other, involve everyone, criticise constructively, disagree politely, keep each other up to the mark (e.g. not let each other resort to English the minute the teacher is not there) and not move on till everyone has finished.

We have been concerned about the learner who just copies, the learner who just rushes to finish, groups who don't work well simply because they don't gel, and the tendency for boys to work competitively or to behave badly and impede the girls' learning.

Marian Carty &
Vee Harris

We have a video of a student teacher in a science lesson arranging for learners in groups to be asked what they think is necessary for a group to work well together and to draw up a contract which they all sign. We give these instructions to our third year:

You will be doing the activities in groups and it is important that you all work well together. You should choose a group leader. Some groups may want to keep the same leader from week to week. Others may want to have a different member of the group taking the responsibility each week.

What the group leader should do

1. collect enough worksheets for the group from the teacher's table
2. explain to the others what to do
3. check if there is a self-marking answer sheet and go through the answers with the group
4. tick off each activity on the activity checklist when it is done
5. make sure everyone in the group helps each other
6. make sure everyone in the group copies down new words
7. keep the noise level down
8. make sure all the worksheets are tidied away at the end of the lesson

What the group should do

1. help each other - ask two people before asking the teacher
2. work as a team
3. aim for a higher standard
4. encourage each other to have a go at talking French as much as possible
5. not just give people your answers but explain how you knew what to put
6. make a list of rules for your group, like this example

Our own rules

1. No bossing.
2. Give everyone their chance to speak.
3. Help each other
4. Work hard
5. Dont mess around and distract other people
6. Give people a chance to express their ideas
7. Work quietly
8. Aim for complete work
9. Wait for others to finish
10. Be in the lesson as much as possible

How can I help them work without me?

Marian Carty & Vee Harris

In the course of our work with teachers, we have become increasingly convinced that time taken to explain to the learners what they are going to be doing, how to do it and why, is time well spent. We cannot assume that somehow they will automatically acquire the social skills that will allow them to work together successfully or the study skills that they need to make use of dictionaries, decode instructions, draft and redraft their work, etc. We need to make these skills explicit and build in activities that give pupils the opportunities to learn them.

Details of activities to foster these skills are given under:

How do I get the groups to work together collaboratively? (page 52)
How do I help them decode instructions? (page 58)
How do I teach them to use dictionaries? (page 61)
How do I teach them to use equipment? (page 58)

It can be helpful to use a checklist such as the one below when introducing a new way of working for the first time. This allows you to talk through the issues and to give study and social skills an equal status to linguistic skills. It can also be used by the pupils to monitor their own progress. On one occasion, we noticed that some pupils were not organising their work sensibly and others were failing to support weaker members of their group. So we spent a lesson discussing the checklist and inviting pupils to comment on what had been achieved so far. In the subsequent lessons many of these problems disappeared.

A chance to look back and consider how you got on.

√√ = I have done this a lot
√ = I have done this a bit
X = I have not done this much

Learning to learn by myself

I have used my common sense to guess what words mean	√√
I have thought if the words look like English words	√
I have looked words up in the dictionary or in the back of the textbook	√√
I have played the tape back to listen again to what I haven't understood	√√

When talking:

I have practised saying any new words out loud	X
I have kept the conversation going even if it meant using mimes or a few English words	√

When writing:

I have made a note of new words	X
I have read over my work to spot mistakes	√

Working with a partner/in groups

To work well as a team together we have:

asked each other for help rather than the teacher	✓
made sure everyone understands before moving on	✓
made sure one person doesn't do all the talking	✓✓
not just copied somebody's answer, but asked them why	✓
checked each other's work when the answers aren't in the back	✗

Organising my learning

I have kept my 'Feuille de progrès' up to date	✓
I'm careful to do the exercises in the best order	✓
I have collected examples of my best work	✗
I plan ahead	✓
I do a lot of listening at home	✓✓
I practise 'Talkbacks' with a partner each week	✓
I work at a good speed for me	✓
I'm now working more quickly through the book	✓

How do I help pupils work on the specific areas they find hard?

Marian Carty &
Vee Harris

As teachers we are able to identify what activities are particularly helpful for developing different skills. We know, for example, that pelmanism games with word cards can help pupils' reading skills and the retention of new vocabulary. Again, we can make this knowledge explicit to the learner and suggested activities can be written up on posters around the classroom. Some teachers give time in their lessons for learners to work in this way on their own weaknesses. Heather Rendall uses the following kind of lists with her classes.

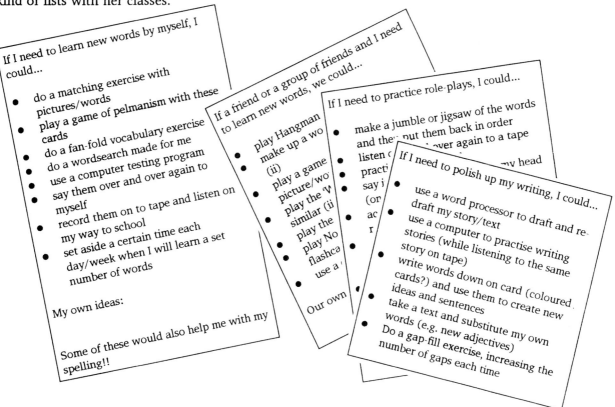

How do I get learners to use the foreign language in pairs/group work?

This is a difficult one which can never be completely resolved. Some teachers have evolved a contract system - the teacher and the learners discuss as a first activity how they are going to work and what the general objectives are. Out of this comes the inescapable logical conclusion that it's common sense for the learners to try to speak as much foreign language as possible. They are, after all, playing the game in the group not in order to play the game but in order to learn the foreign language. There's not much point if it is all done in English. Most groups are willing to accept this commonsense argument. However, they know that they don't always have the language for what they want to say so they must be encouraged to look things up, ask questions and occasionally use English words in foreign language sentences. There is no harm in using an 'interlanguage' provided it is a step towards the objective and not accepted as an end in itself. It is important not to be dogmatic but to be encouraging. It is after all not surprising that learners use English particularly when they do not have the foreign language for what they want to say.

In a game there could be a second way of gaining points. Each time players use the target language for things like 'now it's your turn', 'pass me the dice, please', they can pick up a special counter. These then count towards winning in the end.

At the end of an activity - game, assignment, computer exercise - the group should reflect on what words in the foreign language they needed and didn't know. These can be collected and put on a poster for subsequent use by them and other groups.

The process starts with the teacher. All standard classroom management can be done in the foreign language. It has to be taught. Posters on the walls showing the most common phrases needed help and/or a list can be kept in exercise books and added to as the need arises - a sort of phrase book for classroom use.

The teacher should always use the foreign language in the classroom except in extreme situations - English should be a very last resort not the first one. With learners it is quite possible to carry on two language conversations in the early stages - the teacher speaks in the foreign language, the learner in English. Gradually learners acquire the language to cope as well. As was said above this often applies in group work too. Learners can move from English to a mixture of English and foreign language and then to the foreign language alone.

We must all remember that, sadly, the evidence we have still shows that in a majority of the foreign language classrooms in this country teachers speak English most of the time. It is not surprising that the learners follow suit.

How do I know what each individual is doing?

The key tool in all independent learning systems is the learner's diary. These take many forms but basically they include what the learner's objective was, what she did in each class and for each homework, what she intends to do next. The diaries may have an entry for each day or each week and cover a half or whole term (examples are on pages 30-31). In the early stages these diaries can be supplemented with 'I can ...' lists of varying sophistication (see the example of a *Carte-échelon* from the Durham Graded Objectives Scheme). In most experiences recounted in this book there are mentions of topic/task lists which have to be ticked by individuals or groups as work is completed.

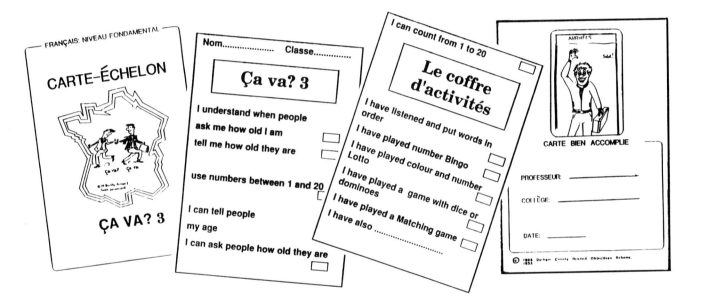

How do I make sure they are not time-wasting, either willfully or unintentionally?

Learners' diaries should be inspected regularly. In class-time the teacher is usually free to move from group to group and keep an eye on things. Unintentional effort wasters are often more difficult to deal with as they may be conscientiously working hard in their view and can resent suggestions that they are not being effective. On the other hand, some learners need a time-out period when they are less intensively occupied. This should be respected. Tact and sensitivity are required.

How do I deal with the reluctant/destructive learner?

In the end there will always be some. It is true, however, that all teachers who use independent learning approaches report an improvement in discipline and a greater willingness on the part of previously reluctant learners. The learner's diary does make objectives explicit and they are decided on by the learner herself. If she fails to meet them she is failing her own challenge, not anyone else's. If learners are finding it genuinely difficult then they have perhaps set themselves too high an objective and need to be more realistic. Disruptive learners have either to be contained by a strong group or isolated to work on their own.

How do I help them decode instructions?

All classroom management language, and that includes the language of instructions in textbooks and worksheets, has to be taught. One teacher gives a lesson on instructions explaining to pupils how to look for clues in the title and identify key instruction words like *soulignez*. She gets learners to design exercises, assignments and worksheets themselves to see how it is done. Learners can also devise instructions for playing a game they already know, like rounders, *Monopoly*, etc. In the early stages, posters on the walls carrying the major phrases and lists in exercise books are helpful. Class and group exercises in finding out what has to be done should be regular activities. Learners should also learn to help each other.

How do I teach them to use equipment?

The best way is to let them teach each other. There is always someone in the class who can operate the machine. What is important is to get them to respect the machines and not mishandle them. They should be taught to treat them gently and any signs of rough handling should be dealt with instantly. A torrent of indignant (and, to the learner, scarcely comprehensible) foreign language can have a dramatic effect.

How do I fit in my input?

How much input does the teacher really need? Some would say much less than others. Some teachers like to introduce the topic themselves. Others leave this to tape, handout or textbook. Frequently, teacher input is needed in the middle of an activity when problems have arisen rather than at the beginning. Sometimes this can be done as a whole class activity but it is often more appropriate to do it with each group as the need arises. In any case, learners should be made aware that teacher input can be called on at any time. The best sort of input arises from learner demand.

Vee Harris   Vee Harris has worked with a group of teachers on this point. She writes:

Most of the teachers felt that they would not wish just to have pupils working in groups. They see whole class input as continuing to be important at beginnings and ends of lessons. At the start of the lesson, pupils need to know what activities are available and what they are about. At the end of the lesson, the teacher may need to 'pull it all together', dealing with:

- what each group has done, how well they have worked: 'You may not have finished but you've worked hard today'. As one teacher commented: 'Teachers have tended to keep that sort of thing to themselves';

- common mistakes or problems that have arisen;

- what words they remember from today;

- role-plays that a sample of pupils act out;

- who has made an effort to use the target language.

Whole class input is also useful to:

- help pupils organise their learning - introduce and explain strategies which will help them learn more effectively;

- clarify and provide appropriate practice of points which may be particularly hard;

- provide oral practice - this is particularly important since many of the group work activities rely on reading or writing and there is a concern about mispronunciation;

- provide variety in lessons. One teacher reported that pupils were more receptive to a whole class input on a Friday afternoon, because (a) it was not the usual way of working, and (b) they had experienced for themselves some of the things that were difficult and felt a need for clarification and explanation.

Clearly, factors like the length of the lesson and the amount of curriculum time are important. Some teachers who only have one very long double period prefer to use the first third, say, for whole class input.

How do I learn not to interfere?

Usually with difficulty. Most teachers have an urge to teach and feel guilty if they are not being constantly active in the classroom. Independent learning means a change of mode by both teacher and learner. The teacher has to let go and allow the learners to learn. If that means doing very little in the classroom then that is what should happen. The teacher's main work is in negotiating appropriate objectives to start with, in providing and producing materials, in guiding learners to work on their own, in being a facilitator in the classroom (which includes judging the right moment to provide appropriate input) and in monitoring and assessing progress.

How do learners access a textbook?

As was said earlier the learner should see the textbook as a tool, not a master. Textbooks need demystifying. None of them is perfect. Why should the learners not look at them critically as well? Encourage them to do an exercise and then say whether it was any good. What would be a better one? Suggestions for getting into a textbook are described in the answer to the first question in this chapter. Ways to help learners approach any written text are described on pages 65-68.

How do I organise free reading?

There are several long-standing and well-established systems. The main question to decide is whether you want proof of something having been read and if so how much. The other problem is that free reading has been a casualty of new approaches to teaching and there are therefore not nearly as many readers on the market as there were twenty years ago. Get copies, either single or in twos and threes, of as many as you can (*Bibliobus* is a good start). Keep them in a library box or on a shelf. Learners can then go and get one whenever they feel like it.

Free reading can be part of their self-selected objectives at various times. In that case it is entered in their diary as an activity to do and what they read is entered as what they have done.

Proof of reading can be done in various ways.

● Comprehension questions. Usually dull and boring for all concerned. What they amount to is a statement 'I can't trust you actually to read this on your own so I'll ask you some questions about it to make sure'. Teachers' questions by definition concern what the teacher thinks is important in the story and are not necessarily what the learner thought important or found interesting. If you believe in comprehension questions get the learners themselves to devise them. You can then discuss both their questions and their answers with them.

● Reviews. Learners write a short review saying whether they found the story entertaining, and if so why or why not, with suggestions for improvement. Reviews can first be written in English but learners should be encouraged to write as much foreign language as they can, even if that means odd words and sentences embedded in otherwise English text. These islands of foreign language gradually expand until it is the foreign language that predominates. Success is when the weakest manages a few foreign language words in an English text. A complete sentence is a triumph. It is on these small beginnings that real proficiency is built.

● Free reading can lead on to rewriting, rewriting as a play subsequently recorded or video taped, or class/group discussion based on the reviews. Be careful, however. On the whole, free reading should be free i.e. reading for pleasure and not necessarily leading to any other sort of outcome at all. It is the very experience of reading for fun without the pressure to produce something from it that is important in the end. The book in the Pathfinder series *Reading for pleasure in the foreign language* (by Ann Swarbrick, CILT, 1990) contains many suggestions and a useful reading diary (see below).

Following from the Pathfinder book on reading for pleasure, we have bought a variety of modern readers in France and in Germany. I am now in the process of colour-coding them for different levels and designing an activity sheet for each book. I do not intend to write a vocabulary list as this will be the learners' responsibility as well as giving their opinions and a short *précis* in English and in the target language. I intend to provide a key in French for the opinion section as well as a framework for the *résumé*, i.e. *Il s'agit de ...* etc as the Pathfinder book suggests.

Christiane Montlibert

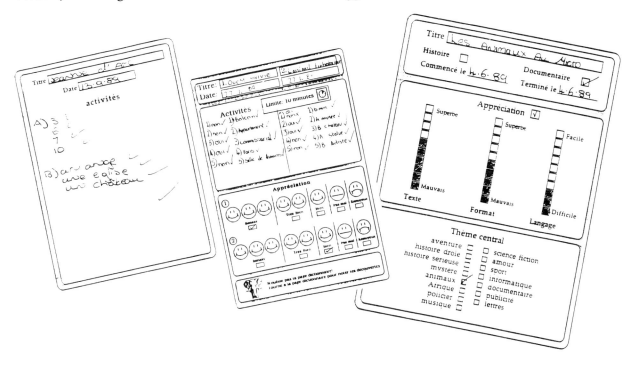

How do I teach them to use dictionaries?

It depends what learners are to start with. They have to learn a series of conventions: alphabetical order, abbreviations like *a* and *n* and *v* (for adjective, noun, verb) etc. They don't necessarily need to know what an adjective, noun or verb is in grammatical terms but only that the abbreviations signal different types of word from which they must make a correct choice. In order to familiarise themselves with them, learners should do exercises involving working from the foreign language to English so that context and common sense guide them to the correct choice.

Working from English to the foreign language is much more dangerous. When they need to do it they should always check back, e.g. if they looked up English *tree* and found French *arbre* they must then look up *arbre* to see if it really means *tree*. This will help with a word like bank, when checking back will give them a clue about whether the word they have got is to do with money or a river.

The important thing is that practice exercises in using a dictionary and a grammar are necessary if wasted time and frustration are to be avoided. It is time well spent.

Unfortunately, there are not many dictionaries about which are constructed with a learner's needs in mind. You only have to look at the several dictionaries recently published for learners of English as a foreign language to realise what we foreign language teachers have not got. Picture dictionaries intended for young native speaker children can also be helpful (see appendix 'Materials and resources' for details of dictionaries).

How can I deal with everyone wanting to ask me things at once?

Becoming an independent learner means learning to find out for yourself. Learners must learn to consult textbooks, vocabulary lists, dictionaries, grammars, and make intelligent deductions from material they are working with. They must consult each other and learn to work together so that all knowledge is pooled. Leni Dam has a set of ten commandments for her class (see her chapter in *Autonomy in language learning*, CILT, 1990). One of them is 'ask three people before you ask me'. They then make a list of things to ask so that if they have to ask the teacher they can deal with several things at one time instead of coming back again and again. Learning to learn also means learning to organise.

How do I prepare for GCSE?

See Alison Orr (page 10), Steven Fawkes (page 18), Hilary Norris Evans (page 21).

How do I monitor progression?

It first depends on what you mean by progression. If preparing for GCSE, then presumably there are topics to be covered and skills to be given adequate practice. Learners check progress through these by their diaries. They should keep a folder of work done and every so often (each half term?) compare what they are doing with what they were doing half a term previously and comment on their progress, e.g. 'I used to find listening to the tapes a bit difficult, now I am finding it easier'; 'the things I am writing now are better/more accurate/longer/more interesting than what I was writing six weeks ago'; 'I haven't made much progress in talking, I must ask what I can do to improve'.

If working with earlier classes, then some sort of learning objectives have to be agreed with the class or group so that they know what they are working towards. It is important for objectives to be differentiated.

Evaluation is an important part of independent learning. It can be started in quite a small way. Mabel Renny (Keith Grammar School, Banffshire) started by giving out a sheet at the end of lessons for second years to fill in. They had to put what they had done, how they had done it, what they intended to do for homework, how they had liked it. She found it a great motivator. They were very honest about what they were achieving. She asked them to write down what she should write on their report card and what their grade and effort mark should be. She then negotiated with them individually about what in fact should be written. There was not much amendment needed as the learners were pretty accurate.

How do I plan a learning programme?

To some extent this was answered in the previous question.

At the beginning it may be a matter of loosening up the scheme of work you already have so that learners can do things in an order of their own choice. As your system becomes more sophisticated, the learning programme can be a matter of negotiation with the class. It will help for classes to have the National Curriculum requirements posted on the classroom wall, to discuss them in relation to language learning, and to arrive at conclusions about how they, the learners, can best satisfy the requirements. All this takes time and teachers must not worry if they have spent a week working out with the class what they are going to do rather than getting on with 'real' language teaching. The result will be much more effective learning in the end.

How do I manage resources?

See Alison Orr (page 10), Margaret Tumber (page 14), Steven Fawkes (page 18) in Chapter 2.

Christiane Montlibert

Most of the presentation I do targets the whole class and I use carousels to extend and consolidate. My TVEI time this year (two hours a week) is used to make up activity cards with differentiated tasks, mounted on cardboard and laminated. I use stars to show the level of difficulty: *easy, **more demanding, ***stretching. The cards are stored in big red cardboard files under topics, which can also accommodate cassettes (C20) and can be carried around easily. According to suitability, the cards are skill-based or mixed-skills. The carousel can start immediately and *mots-clefs* are provided to enable more independence from the teacher as well as from the textbook used, which is *Francoscope* and is too difficult for some of our slow learners. My collection of tasks comes from *Toi & moi, Au secours, Read it in French, GCSE letter writing, Allez-y, Signposts French*, etc.

What happens when a group finishes?

In one sense this should not happen as differentiated objectives should mean there is always something to move on to. However, one must avoid the treadmill effect and give groups the feeling that they have in fact finished and therefore arrived somewhere. There are also the odd five minutes at the end of a lesson when groups/individuals will have completed a particular section of work and it is not worth starting the next bit. These situations should be recognised by the learners and dealt with appropriately. They can become teachers and prepare activity cards or games or start 'reading for pleasure'. Fill-in activities should be noted in the diary: 'Today my group finished what we wanted to do so we made a crossword to put in the games box/completed a crossword/read a library book/I helped Sandra finish her piece.' There might also be an entry 'I was told off for causing a disturbance/for stopping Sandra working'.

What about the National Curriculum requirements in creative writing, awareness of language and the treatment of cross-curricular themes?

Since autonomy is at least as much an attitude to learning as an organisational approach, it follows that it is appropriate for the learning implied in these requirements. Christiane Montlibert's work with her classes at Boswells School reported in Chapter 3 deals with all three of these points.

Creative writing

By its very nature this assumes an individual or at least a small group approach where each individual can have a direct input. Collaborative productions have enormous advantages. Each group member, however weak, can and should contribute something and the resources of all help to reduce the number of inaccuracies. And, not the least important, the teacher has only six compositions to mark instead of thirty and so can give them much more attention. Modest steps to start with might be the expansion, extension and redrafting of given stories or incidents, devising different endings, adding events, writing them down from the point of view of different participants. In all cases learners need to review their repertoire of vocabulary and grammar, make lists of what they know already that is relevant and what they want to know. The important difference from the usual approach, however, is that instead of the preparation being done as a whole class activity resulting in thirty pieces of work that are essentially the same, the preparation is done by individuals or small groups using the teacher as a guide and a resource.

Being creative by Barry Jones (CILT Pathfinder Series, 1992) gives many suggestions for creative strategies and activities.

Awareness of language

Learners should be encouraged to make notes of pieces of language they find interesting and which will help them express themselves more clearly and accurately. Sometimes these will be straightforward pieces of vocabulary, sometimes they will relate to grammatical rules (why do the French say ONU and OTAN when we say UNO and NATO?), sometimes to usage (what happens to the French equivalent of 'brown' when describing eyes, shoes, hair?), sometimes to pronunciation (how would Germans, Spaniards, French pronounce the names of the people in the group and why?). Old-fashioned grammar lessons can be interesting if they are asked for and taught by members of the class themselves, as Christiane Montlibert shows (see page 32). In all cases it is what learners ask for and find out which is more likely to stick in their minds than notes dictated by the teacher.

A good example is Christiane Montlibert's environment project described on page 39. The important principle to bear in mind is, as Lid King said: 'It is possible to teach "real" subjects (in the foreign language) to groups below the age of 16'. The more learners are able to exercise choice the more they are likely to find the subject interesting and relevant. All that of course has to be qualified by the availability of materials and other resources. You should remember, however, that teachers of other subjects may also have materials in foreign languages and/or be competent enough themselves in the language to be able to give considerable help.

Cross-curricular themes

How can learners get into a text?

CILT organised a course on post-16 work in languages and Lid King writes about some of the ideas that came out of it.

One of the perennial difficulties of text exploitation is the effort required of the teacher in both selecting a range of suitable texts and in devising different and engaging activities. At the same time the learner is often uninterested in the end product of our efforts. Why not, therefore, both **reduce** the time needed for teacher preparation (the Sunday night panic in front of a blank sheet of paper), and at the same time **increase** the involvement of the learner in the process? Might such an approach not merely enable the teacher to remain sane but also lead to more effective learning?

Lid King

This was the premise on which the following notes are based. They arise from the deliberations of a group of post-16 teachers, but they are linked to our individual experiences both before and after the event. Many of the points are relevant to all levels of language learning, but they seem to have particular importance for the learner with some foundation (linguistic and conceptual) on which to build.

Our aim was not so much to provide a list of new techniques for the harassed teacher, but to suggest that by shifting the emphasis of work in the classroom from her to the learner, **any** technique could become more effective and enjoyable for both parties. What follows therefore is not a prescription but an example of what might be possible whatever your own favourite learning/teaching activities.

The starting point may be extremely banal. In one case there was a Friday afternoon lesson with a polite but not very co-operative sixth form group comprising two antagonistic groups and a rather more apathetic middle one. The teacher was unprepared! All he had was a text which appeared to be of a suitable level. No time to prepare questions, so in desperation he asked the class (individually and then in groups) to devise questions on various sections of the text. Next, 'best' questions were selected.

Groups put their questions to the other groups. Marks were awarded out of five. Since two groups disliked each other, full marks were rarely given, but then justifications had to be made. The boring unprepared lesson became a favourite one.

Such a happy accident suggests how to proceed. We should perhaps try to change standard activities by involving learners in the process of grappling with the text rather than digesting it for them.

For example:

When preparing a text

Instead of	Try
• *Telling pupils what it is about* *or* *Giving background information*	• Getting learners to predict content. Base this on headlines or images, for example. It could be a group activity, individual or brainstorm. If necessary, support can be given (see *Images of violence* below).
• *Telling them why it's useful*	• Discussing the students' own predictions and opinions.
• *Giving key vocabulary*	• Asking students to list vocabulary already known on the given theme; and Getting learners to find unknown vocabulary which may be useful, using dictionary, *assistante*, teacher. Giving students concepts and ideas in the foreign language which also appear in the text, and asking them to write or prepare a possible version of what the text will be about - for later comparison (see *Inventing a story* below).

Images of violence

IMAGES DE LA VIOLENCE

Exercice 1.1 - Travail à deux

Regardez attentivement les images (a) à (e). A tour de rôle, et à l'aide du vocabulaire ci-dessous, décrivez chacune des images à votre partenaire.

Dans l'image on voit / on dirait...
Il semble que...
Je pense que c'est...
C'est peut-être...
L'homme porte...
Par terre il y a ...
La dame / jeune personne semble...
Il / elle a l'air...

L'image m'émeut / me laisse indifférent / me révolte / me répugne/ m'attriste / me désespère...

L'image est...
violente	déchirante
choquante	révoltante
absurde	incroyable

Exercice 1.2 - Travail à deux

Avec votre partenaire, faites une liste des différents aspects de la violence qu'on peut voir dans ces cinq images, et trouvez un titre pour chacune d'entre elles.

Source: *Bridging the gap: GCSE to 'A' Level* by John Thorogood and Lid King (CILT, 1991)

Inventing a story

Preparatory task: make up a story from a jumble of phrases

Working in pairs or small groups, invent a story using as many as possible of the following phrases:

ambas de 25 años - tras tomar unas copas - dos mujeres que sirvieron de gancho - en la calle Valvrede de Madrid - le dejaron en libertad - la policía arrestó a las dos parejas - un cuarto de hora - según informa - robar dinero, ropa y un reloj - dos hombres - intimidaron al visitante - llevaron a cabo el asalto

Read the authentic text

Now read the following article and compare it with your own story.

Dos mujeres llevaron a un hombre a su casa para robarle
El País, **Madrid**

Dos mujeres que sirvieron de *gancho,* y otros dos hombres que llevaron a cabo el asalto, fueron detenidos ayer acusados de robar dinero, ropa y un reloj a un hombre de 46 años, según informa la Jefatura Superior de Policía de Madrid.

María Nieves Cabrera y Dolores Monge Guillén, ambas de 25 años, conocieron en la calle Valverde de Madrid a un hombre al que tras tomar unas copas con él, le llevaron a una casa de la barriada del Pozo del Huevo, en Entrevías. Cuando apenas llevaban un cuarto de hora en su interior, siempre de acuerdo con el relato policial, entraron en la casa Miguel Angel González Marcos, de 27, y Francisco Javier Melero Ballesteros, de 26, quienes intimidaron al visitante con un objeto contundente y al que robaron el reloj, una cazadora de cuero, un talonario de cheques y una tarjeta de crédito. Posteriormente le dejaron en libertad.

La policía, tras recibir la llamada del asaltado, hizo un rastreo por la zona y arrestó a las dos parejas, recuperando todo el botín.

(El País, 21.11.87)

Source: *Learning foreign languages from authentic texts* by David Little et al (Authentik in association with CILT, 1989)

When presenting a text

👎 Instead of	👍 Try
• *Explaining / testing vocabulary*	• Asking learners to list words not known or guessed (working in groups will reduce the number of unknowns); then get learners to compare with prepared list, and find out unknown words collaboratively, etc.
• *Devising comprehension questions*	• Getting learners to devise questions (if text is long ask them to do this in groups with part of text).
• *Asking pupils to list/sort key words*	• Getting learners to 'teach' each other 'their' piece of text.

When exploiting a text

👎 Instead of	👍 Try
• *Asking detailed questions on text unseen*	• Involving learners in these and other processes. NB: if stages 1 and 2 have gone well they are already doing this!
• *Devising grammar exercise based on text*	
• *Giving framework for summary*	

When transforming a text

👎 Instead of	👍 Try
• *Setting essays*	• Having a 'graffiti wall' where favourite phrases and words are written.
• *Devising retranslations*	• Encouraging re-use of graffiti.
	• Giving choices of activities - poems, songs, interviews

These examples underline above all the importance of early stages of text exploitation - often underestimated in more 'traditional' communicative approaches. In attempting to help learners progress we have often forgotten that they bring with them a great deal of prior knowledge - of language and of the content matter of the topics we study. The importance of harnessing that prior knowledge cannot be overestimated. It can transform advanced learning from a worthy but often dull pursuit into something dynamic and productive. It can transform the teacher from an exhausted automaton 'revealing' the secrets of the textbook and give her a new role as supporter and director of the learner's progress. By freeing her from often mundane tasks (writing vocabulary lists, comprehension questions) it can enable her to help where help is needed, e.g. the five words which nobody in the class understands, the repeated inaccuracy in expression. Above all, it can change the learner from a polite but bored consumer of predigested worksheets into an active participant in the process of learning.

Chapter 5

PRINCIPLES AND DEFINITIONS

This chapter is in three sections. The first is a series of statements agreed by teachers at the end of the Dyffryn House workshop with explanatory comments. The second summarises the main ideas of a book, *Learner autonomy: definitions, issues and problems* (Authentik, 1991) by David Little, which was written as a result of his preparing the keynote paper for the Lane End conference. The third is the gist of Leni Dam's final talk to the Dyffryn House workshop.

**Learner
autonomy ...**

... is not just self-study/flexible learning;

Both of these assume that the teacher plans the study or learning. An essential part of learner autonomy is that learners choose what to do and how to do it within the frameworks negotiated with the teacher.

... does not exclude collaborative learning;

It is important that autonomous learning does not become isolated learning. Indeed 'independent' learning should be seen as 'interdependent' learning, i.e. an essential part of it is learning in groups, helping others and being helped oneself by fellow learners as well as the teacher.

*... involves learner choice/freedom, the possibility of negotiation, responsibility
for one's learning and awareness of one's own role in the process;*

Negotiation does not mean the teacher abdicates and learners do what they like. It takes two to negotiate. What it does mean is that the learner understands and accepts external constraints like syllabuses and examination requirements, and teachers accept that learners can have a legitimate view about how best to go about learning. Autonomy means learners choose the way that suits them best.

... involves collaboration and a sense of interdependence;

Not only collaboration with peers as was mentioned above, but collaboration with the teacher on what is in the end a joint enterprise. Teachers and learners must move out of their roles as 'givers' and 'receivers' and see themselves as collaborators.

... involves evaluation by the learners themselves;

Awareness of one's own learning processes means not only deciding how best to set about a task but also being fearless in deciding whether the task was well done or not, and how the learning method can be improved next time. If you failed to remember more than half the ten words you had decided to learn, what are you going to do to improve your result next time?

... implies a new view of the teacher's role;

The teacher is no longer there to induce the class, like an orchestral conductor, to carry on whole class activities altogether and all at the same time. The teacher has to realise that 'teaching' does not always lead to 'learning' and that 'learning' is the more important. The question to ask is not 'how am I going to teach this?' but 'how are they going to learn this?'. That means giving the learners freedom within the constraints of available resources and teaching conditions to decide how to organise their own learning. The teacher is there to advise and to see that each learner does in fact face up to his/her responsibilities.

... implies a new view of the learner's role;

Learners do not immediately know what to do. Most have been conditioned to behave like small birds in the nest and wait for the teacher to come along and drop them a worm. Now they have to learn to find the worms for themselves, with the teacher giving plenty of support and suggesting where and how - when asked. Learners must also learn to ask: to ask each other, to interrogate resources (dictionaries, grammars, reference books, databases), to understand instructions and to formulate questions for the teacher in order to get the most information economically. This does not come easily; the learners have to learn to be independent learners. They have to learn that they have an active role to play in learning. Teachers need to make the system explicit to learners. Jan Fornachon, in a sixth form college (Barton Peveril College, Eastleigh), reported one of her learners saying: 'Miss, when are you going to teach us?'.

... implies a new view of error;

We have already arrived at a new view of error in the general move towards communicative competence. On the whole this has meant: don't worry about making mistakes, have a go - if you manage to communicate what you intended to, then you have succeeded. This was a necessary step to take after the years of struggling to write grammatically correct sentences and losing one mark for each mistake (half for accents!). But it has its own dangers. The major one is that learners are satisfied with a sort of pidgin which doesn't exist as a language in the real world of native-speaker users at all.

The new view of error must now be that learners do continue to have a go without inhibition and that raw communication of messages continues to be rewarded as a useful skill, but learners must be aware that real people don't speak/write like that. Errors should be seen as necessary steps in learning a language, positive indicators of where you need to work next. It is not a matter of 'doing the corrections' but of looking at errors and deciding why they are wrong.

People who don't make mistakes don't make anything, but people who don't look at their mistakes and learn from them don't make progress.

... is not an answer to teacher shortage.

Learner autonomy does not mean that the teacher's work is less, but that it changes. In the classroom there is undoubtedly less 'teaching' to be done in the traditional manner, though whole class teaching does not necessarily disappear altogether. In the classroom the teacher will be working with groups, answering questions, checking the records, dealing with individual problems, but **not interfering**. Outside the classroom the keeping and checking of records and preparation of materials will still go on. Teachers involved report that the workload is not less but that it is less stressful, less demanding of nervous energy, more enjoyable and more productive. Any suggestion from managers that 'now that they are working on their own you can look after sixty instead of thirty, can't you' must be firmly squashed.

At the Lane End conference we were fortunate in having both David Little (Director of the Centre for Language and Communication Studies, Trinity College, Dublin) and Leni Dam (In-service teacher trainer at the Royal Danish School of Educational Studies) to talk to us. Both are internationally renowned authorities on learner autonomy.

David Little gave the keynote talk which he later expanded into a book: *Learner autonomy: definitions, issues and problems* (Authentik, 1991). The following are summaries of some of the points he makes. The book itself should be read for the supporting argument and explanation.

- It is not just a new methodology, but a new approach.

What autonomy is not

- It is not just self-instruction, i.e. learning without a teacher necessarily being present.

- It does not require the teacher to give up all initiative and control.

- Autonomous learners do not make teachers redundant.

Implications for language teaching

Knowledge is presented by teachers but it is learnt by learners - either superficially as someone else's knowledge to be regurgitated for exercises and examinations, or more completely if it is absorbed by being used for the learner's own purposes. Effective and worthwhile learning may actually then depend on the extent to which learners achieve autonomy.

The main goal of foreign language teaching has been to enable learners to use the language as a medium of communication. Communications occur in a vast range of circumstances and situations. Communicative efficiency therefore depends on learners achieving a substantial degree of autonomy as language users.

Two classrooms

Little illustrates the difference between teacher-imposed knowledge and learner-assimilated knowledge with a description of two contrasting classes which deserves complete quotation.

'A description of two classrooms may help to show just how far it is necessary to depart from traditional patterns of classroom organisation in order to enable language learners to become autonomous language users.

Classroom 1

In the first classroom, where the target language is German, the teacher is testing the learners' comprehension of an authentic text dealing with environmental pollution, which they had to read for homework last night. She gradually works her way round the class until every learner has answered a question. After each answer she provides evaluation, feedback and reinforcement, often reformulating the answer in several different ways. She also draws attention to certain formal features of the target language, not only in response to learners' mistakes but also when something in the text reminds her of an area of likely difficulty. German is spoken the whole time, and for the most part the learners' answers are not only factually correct but also well-formed. Why, then, does this classroom leave such a profoundly non-communicative impression? And why, after the class, do several learners express dissatisfaction with the process they have just been through? For one thing, a whole-class activity in which the teacher asks questions and individual pupils are nominated to reply clearly fails to engage the sustained attention of all the learners. The observer notices that most learners show signs of wandering attention from time to time, and some of their replies to the teacher's questions do not immediately attach themselves to the thread of the lesson. For another thing, every utterance that the learners produce is generated out of the text they have in front of them, which acts as a prompt. If the text were taken away, what exactly would remain? But perhaps most important of all, the learners clearly do not feel that they have any particular stake in what is going on. The text they are working on was certainly not their choice, and most of them seem to find difficulty in showing even a polite interest in it. They can perform an externally imposed task with a fair measure of competence, but one senses that they would have considerable difficulty in going beyond the task to a more flexible use of the language that it contains.

Classroom 2

In the second classroom, where the target language is English, the learners are working in five groups, with between three and five learners in each group. They are nearing the end of a four-week period during which each group has been engaged on a project of its own devising. Two of the projects seem to run counter to communicative orthodoxy, for they involve translation from the mother tongue into the target language - one group is translating a fairy tale into English with a view to subsequently rewriting it as a short radio play; the other group, fascinated by recent developments in Rumania, is compiling a report in English by translating extracts from a collection of Danish newspaper articles. The teacher moves from group to group, discussing progress, suggesting how some difficulty might be overcome, indicating where information on a particular topic can be found, and providing explanations in response to direct questions about the target language. Despite the apparently traditional activities that some of the groups are involved in, this second classroom makes an infinitely more communicative impression than the first one. It is not simply that the learners are speaking English to one another (something that the teacher has insisted on from the beginning). The essential point of difference is that they are communicating meanings that clearly matter to them. Because their projects are entirely of their own devising, they are deeply interested in what they are doing; even obviously weaker pupils are fully involved. These learners are autonomous in the sense that they have determined the content of their learning, decided how they should go about the series of tasks their project imposes on them, and accepted responsibility collectively and individually for reviewing their progress. Thus they experience the learning they are engaged on as their own, and this enables them to achieve to a remarkable degree the autonomy that characterises the fluent language user. The fact that they make more or less steady progress in their language learning allows us to suppose that this autonomy helps to activate and nourish their unconscious acquisition processes.

In the first of our two classrooms it is the teacher who determines the content of her pupils' learning. No doubt she would argue that the authentic text on which her class is based is intrinsically interesting, so that her learners ought to find it stimulating. But she evidently made no effort to engage their prior interest in the theme of environmental pollution - for example, by having a 'brainstorming' session in which learners could all contribute to a preliminary lexical exploration of the topic. And the discourse structure that she imposes on the class does not allow individual learners to contribute anything of their own. Because it restricts the learners to a peripheral role in the discourse, the approach does nothing to engage their own personal construct systems.

Engaging learners' personal constructs

In the second classroom, by contrast, everything is done by techniques of negotiation that encourage learners to explore and make explicit their personal constructs. That is not to say that the teacher is not in control. On the contrary, the learners are expected to follow a set of disciplined procedures - they must determine in general terms what they want to do; specify the end-product (usually a written or tape-recorded text); determine what materials they need in order to achieve their aims; and make sure that each member of the group is given a role which enables him or her to contribute fully to the project in all its phases. Moreover, each learner is expected to keep a diary in English which maintains a record of individual and group progress and evaluates how well the individual learner and the group have worked. The teacher begins each lesson with five minutes or so in which she talks to the class as a whole (in English), reminding them of their targets, encouraging groups to talk to one another about their progress, and answering any general questions. It is an important feature of this approach that at the end of each project-phase of four or five weeks the learners must form new groups. This prevents the establishment of cliques, ensures that in the course of a school year each learner works at least once with all the other members of the class, and insists on maintaining the class as a single open society.'

The textbook

To the extent that a textbook defines the content of learning and so imposes meanings on learners that they may not find relevant to them, it can get in the way of efficient language learning. The 'tyranny of the coursebook' can be overcome in various ways:

- supplementation with authentic materials that give learners some choice;

- getting learners to use the coursebook to teach each other;

- replacing the coursebook with materials that teach other parts of the curriculum in the target language.

Learner autonomy and the teacher

A first step is to invite learners to make explicit what they expect from the learning process; the next is a thorough exploration with the learners of the aims of the syllabus and the ways in which the learners can make those aims their own. This is better than a lecture of the benefits of autonomous learning.

Autonomy cannot be achieved without changing the roles of the teacher and the learner. Teachers have to move away from the idea that if they are not 'teaching' (which usually means talking) then the learners can't be learning. It is when learners are talking that they are likely to be learning.

Warning!

Even teachers who encourage their pupils to learn by discovering for themselves often find it difficult not to intervene when they see learners, individually or in a group, grappling with a problem and moving only slowly towards a solution. But it is precisely the grappling - the grinding together of conflicting constructs - that leads to learning, and much learner effort will be wasted if the teacher intervenes too quickly.

Sharing the burden

For a teacher to commit himself to learner autonomy requires a lot of nerve, not least because it requires him to abandon any lingering notion that he can somehow guarantee the success of learners by his own effort. Instead he must dare to trust the learners. The expository teacher carries the whole burden of learning on his own shoulders: one of the chief reasons for trying to develop learner autonomy is to get the learners to share the burden.

Learner autonomy and the learner

Learners should be encouraged to accept responsibility for their learning as early as possible. Most of the necessary techniques have been in common use in primary schools for many years.

Many pupils feel comfortable in a state of more or less total dependence on the teacher. It is not surprising if some of them resist the idea of autonomy. As a rule, the older the learners are when they first meet the idea of autonomy, the harder it is likely to be for the teacher to convince them that it makes sense.

Learning materials

There should be a compromise between learner-selected and teacher-selected materials arising from the need to accommodate both learner choice and the teacher's special expertise derived from greater knowledge and experience. The content of learning should therefore be subject to negotiation and continuous review. Learners need access to information about the target language - dictionaries, grammars, etc - and need to be taught how to use them. They need more input than is usual under other learning approaches but this does not depend on providing a great wealth of materials. A single issue of one of the *Authentik* newspapers contains more input than many coursebooks (see appendix 'Materials and resources' for details of Authentik).

Training the learner

- Learning to learn is central. Learners have to be able to reflect critically on their learning, evaluate their progress and, if necessary, make adjustments to their methods of learning.

- Keeping a diary helps learners to give shape to their learning but can lead to fairly general statements. They need guidance in identifying learning strategies and evaluating their effectiveness.

- Learning a language depends partly on unconscious acquisition and partly on deliberate efforts to remember things one is conscious of wanting to learn.

For the first type of learning there is only one rule: never miss an opportunity to use (listen to, speak, read and write) the language you are learning. Reflect on your performance, note your successes and when difficulties arise try to find out why.

Conscious learning usually concerns vocabulary and grammar. Learning rules is not likely to improve fluency but can improve accuracy where there is time to plan and revise. Vocabulary books can be useful provided they contain words learners have chosen to learn and are reviewed regularly. Conscious learning is more effective if it is organised by the learner.

Getting learners to correct one anothers' work can be highly beneficial; another person's mistakes always seem easier to detect than one's own.

And finally

'I do not believe that learner autonomy offers infallible solutions to every problem encountered in classroom learning; nor do I believe that it guarantees success in every case. But I do believe that it makes sense, not only as the logical outcome of learner-centredness in education generally, but also as the approach to language learning that can best do justice to communicative ideals and the insights we are beginning to gain from empirical research into language acquisition.'

Leni Dam is a teacher of English and teacher trainer of many years standing in Denmark. In spite of her international reputation as an expert she remains firmly rooted in the classroom, where she continues to teach from ten-year-old beginners upwards. She has been practising a fairly advanced form of independent learning for over a decade with enormous success. She rarely uses textbooks but relies heavily on magazines for pictures and texts and on realia often brought in by her learners. She rarely makes complex materials; she has been heard to say 'I have never never spent a weekend making a game for my learners. They can do that themselves'. Her charismatic presence at the Lane End and Dyffryn House conferences inspired all of us. Few of us felt strong enough yet to go as far as she has gone but all of us could see the validity of her approach and the practical results. The maturity and accuracy of the written work of even her first year learners was remarkable.

Her approach is outlined in her contribution to the Lane End conference papers (*Autonomy in language learning*, CILT, 1990) and what she actually does in her classroom will be recounted in a forthcoming book for Authentik (to be published in 1993). In her final few words to the Dyffryn House conference she summed up her philosophy:

All learners are autonomous anyway because they all learn in their own individual ways. They need to learn how to choose and tackle materials, how to learn from each other and how to know what they know and what they don't know. It is important for the teacher to say occasionally 'I think you should do so and so' and not to abdicate responsibility. There must be trust and respect between teacher and learner.

The classroom is an enormous resource and should not be regarded as never as good as the 'real' thing. Similarly, learners should not be seen as somehow defective; they have great resources too that should be respected and used.

Learner autonomy may be an off-putting phrase. It is better to look at the matter more simply. As teachers we should be conscious of what we do and of what learners do, why and how we do things and what we can make of that process. As teachers we should focus on learning rather than teaching - turn things round so that we talk of learning materials rather than teaching materials; think of learning as a long string of experiments, give learners the chance to begin again and again. Learner autonomy is also to be seen as the right of teachers to develop as human beings. Teachers have always said they learn from their pupils. It is time to be more aware of that. It is personal development all the time in negotiation and in combination with learners. We are talking about developing autonomy in ourselves as well as our learners: how we can be better at knowing what we are doing and why, at increasing our own awareness too. It should never stop.

Chapter 6

INDEPENDENT LEARNING IN THE LANGUAGES DEPARTMENT

The following are some suggestions for discussion in languages departments, contributed by Pat McLagan who is a Teacher Liason Officer at CILT and who, as a former advisory teacher, has provided a wide range of INSET on this subject.

Pat McLagan

A developmental profile to be adapted for department use

Where are you now?
Where would you like to be in one year's time?

Most lessons are teacher-dominated
↓
In most lessons there is some pair or group work which is presented and controlled by the teacher
↓
Some efforts are made to develop initiative and independence through individual tasks and small group work
↓
Development of initiative and problem solving are a priority but as yet efforts lack coherence
↓
Time has been devoted to preparation of suitable materials and the preparation of the classroom for more independent work
↓
Time has been devoted to negotiating with learners and developing independent study skills and most learners are now much less dependent on the teacher
↓
For *at least* half the time learners are working independently on tasks and the teacher is acting as tutor
↓
For *at least* half the time learners are working individually or in groups on multi-tasks involving problem solving and initiative

Different teaching and learning needs and skills

As an individual teacher

- Refer to the progress chart on the previous page. Decide approximately where your current practice fits the progression.

- Adapt the statements to fit your own styles and goals if necessary.

- If you want to take the next step, what do you need in order to do it? Refer to *Taking steps to overcome the problems* on pages 81-82.

- Find someone else in your department or school with whom you can collaborate and evaluate success.

As a department

- Refer to the progress chart on the previous page.

- Is it necessary or advisable for all teachers to have the same goals for independent learning?

- Discuss the goals. Adapt them as necessary.

- How can teachers' different talents be used to the full?

- How can the department best support teachers undertaking independent learning?

- In what ways can experience and materials be shared most efficiently?

- How can teachers best support the next stage?

Increasing independent learning

Planning a pilot unit: one suggestion

1. Choose a year group.

2. Choose a unit of work/topic which lends itself to autonomous learning and for which you have a good range of resources.

3. Decide how long you want the pilot to last.

4. Collect together all the materials you have on the topic. Select those which can be used for independent learning. Make sure that there are plenty of materials for listening and speaking practice.

5. Write out:

   a. a core objective/set of objectives;

   b. extension required;

   c. reinforcement required.

6. Organise material into lessons creating supplementary material if necessary to fill gaps.

7. Carry out a pupil evaluation during the pilot and at the end.

8. Discuss the evaluation as a department.

Problems...
Problems...

I would like to develop more independence in my students, but...

I don't have my own classroom and have to carry all my materials and equipment from room to room.

My pupils don't know how to learn without my constant attention.

There are only one or two of us interested in working this way in our department.

We've got few resources - mainly old coursebooks.

I am worried that I will not be able to get round all the pupils to check on what they are doing.

Our classroom doesn't have sufficient power points.

It all seems so daunting!

Many of my pupils have emotional and behavioural difficulties. Often they don't want to work with each other. They also require constant support from me.

Discipline is such a problem - they need me at the front controlling them.

**Taking steps
to overcome
problems**

Some issues for discussion in departments, keeping the ultimate goal as simple as possible.

	1	2	3	GOAL
THE CLASSROOM	Moving from room to room? Can cupboard and wall space be negotiated with other users of the rooms so that you can keep resources in there or set them out before the lesson?	Own room, but other users constantly move furniture? Try to negotiate and come to a compromise. Teachers in other departments may be trying to work in the same way.	Not enough power points? While waiting for the work to be done, invest in a multi-socket cassette player with rechargeable batteries if you can.	**Flexible layout in all modern language classrooms.**
RESOURCES	Is it possible to plan independent work based on any textbook with adaptation? Are there sufficient materials to practise speaking?	How to access the necessary equipment? Listening posts, video and computers are desirable. Good, easy photocopying facilities are important.	Is there a department resource area for sharing and storage? Can you buy small numbers of books and tapes? Can you record onto short cassettes and videos?	**Resources are accessible to learners and meet their different requirements. They are varied and include plenty of materials to encourage speaking.**
TASKS	How should the materials the learners work with now be adapted?	What extra materials are required to create multiskill tasks? Is differentiation predominantly by task or by outcome?	How do the tasks created encourage the use of the target language among learners? Do they encourage problem solving?	**Tasks contain a mix of skills. Instructions are in simple target language. Tasks involve initiative and problem solving where possible.**

	1	2	3	GOAL
STUDY SKILLS	Are learners aware of: ● the aims of the lesson? ● the week's work? ● the term's work?	Is there a department plan on: ● how to use a dictionary? ● how to learn vocabulary? etc	Are learners able to use all the equipment? Whom do they ask if they need help - the teacher or each other?	**A programme for study skills has been planned for the department and for the school as a whole.**
ROLE OF TEACHER AND TUTOR	Teacher or technician? Feel redundant? At everyone's beck and call?	Until class is used to working independently, teacher may have to maintain an overview of the whole class and not be too engrossed in one group.	Teacher's role as animator and facilitator of the use of the target language is crucial and must be planned.	**Individual teacher input to lesson is carefully planned to maximise efficient use of time for efficient learning, concentrating in particular on speaking skills.**
EFFECTIVE GROUP WORK	Groups can waste a lot of time getting started. Try providing progress charts, diaries and deadlines. Negotiate rules Watch them carefully at first.	In classes with learners with emotional and behavioural difficulties, pupils can still develop independence. Collaboration may be slow in coming, but it does not preclude independent working.	Tasks must be crystal clear. Instructions in simple target language. Teacher may need to explain to whole class first.	**Learners work confidently without much prompting by the teacher. They usually respect and accommodate different aptitudes and interests and work increasingly in the target language.**

Conclusion

Learner autonomy and autonomous learning are terms that have now been around for some time but which are in fact tautologies. Every learner in every situation is, strictly speaking, autonomous because only the learner can learn, no-one can do her learning for her. What is meant by autonomous learning is the autonomous organisation of one's learning - learners have at least a hand in what and how they learn. In this sense, complete autonomy is not possible because, as in all human activity, constraints are set by physical circumstances, society's demands and the needs of other equally autonomous learners. What we are about then is how to increase the learners' power for the autonomous organisation of their own learning in order to make it more effective.

Learners organising learning

Distance learning, supported self-study, flexible learning, all increase these powers in some directions though not in others. Distance learning - the Open University is a good example - allows learners to work at their own pace at times they choose within the framework of assessments, tutorial meetings, summer schools and annual examinations. Objectives, materials and assessment procedures are decided by others. Supported self-study and flexible learning usually allow learners some freedom to find their own path through what has to be learnt, though often, in schools at any rate, this has to be done at least partly at set periods in the timetable. They allow learners only limited opportunities to negotiate their own goals, discover their own learning styles and decide how their learning should be evaluated.

At the other end of the continuum, other systems allow learners to decide what they are going to do, how and when they are going to do it and how it is to be assessed. These decisions are usually made collectively at class or group level, underlining the interdependent nature of autonomous learning.

The aim of this book is to suggest ways in which teachers and learners of modern foreign languages can move, in quite small steps, along that continuum to points where they feel comfortable. Why should they do this at all? No evidence is ever conclusive or ever completely indicative of every individual's behaviour, but the evidence suggests that learners are more effective and more willing if they have had a hand in what and how they are to learn. They are also usually honest, not to say hard, on themselves when it comes to self-evaluation. Evidence from records of achievement systems is convincing on that.

There are wider educational reasons too. If we want our learners to become independent thinkers, able and confident enough to do things for themselves, truly democratic citizens in a democratic community, realising the necessity for social co-operation but willing to question, discuss and argue for change, free spirits willing a willingly collaborative community, people who feel they have a stake in their community because they can affect what happens within it, then we must start giving them opportunities to acquire all these skills and attitudes in school. It should be part of their education. As teachers we must not rob our learners of the experience of learning for themselves or of acquiring the skills that such experience gives them.

Letting go - taking hold

It is not just a matter of organisation, however. It requires a change of attitude by both teachers and learners. Learners must no longer sit there and expect to be taught; teachers must no longer stand up there teaching all the time. Teachers have to learn to let go and learners have to learn to take hold. Learners must be seen as having value as learners and not being in some way defective. This change, as far as modern language teachers are concerned, will be as great as the revolution we carried out over the last decade or so when we moved the basis of language teaching away from the mere manipulation of grammar in order to produce well-formed sentences, to the use of language for effective communication in a variety of circumstances.

We must all be aware of course that autonomous learning is not another of those panaceas which is going to solve all our and our learners' problems. The experience of practising teachers illustrated in this book does suggest, however, that autonomous learning systems tend to lead to more teachers and more learners being more successful and more content. That can't be bad.

Appendix

MATERIALS AND RESOURCES

☐ *Authentik* (Authentik Language Learning Resources Materials Ltd, 27 Westland Square, Dublin 2, Ireland)

> A periodical reading and listening resource (five issues a year) for intermediate to advanced students. It consists of a newspaper containing press extracts in the target language, covering a wide range of topics of current interest. Each issue also contains in-depth treatment of one particular topic. Parallel to the newspaper is a cassette containing radio news broadcasts, interviews and features, some specially commissioned, many linked to the newspaper coverage. The package is completed by a *learner's supplement*, printed with the newspaper, which combines a transcript of the recordings with a variety of supplementary activities to exploit the two resources. There is also a separate *Authentik user's guide* available. Versions for **English, French, German** and **Spanish.**

☐ *Bibliobus* (Mary Glasgow, 1982)

> Five boxed sets of graded readers + support material. Aim to encourage extensive individual reading. Collections A and B now also available on cassette.

☐ Bougard M T, P McLagan and M Raddan, *A la carte* (Mary Glasgow, 1982)

> Flexible reading comprehension practice material, for individual, pair and whole class work. Two levels available.

☐ Bray B et al, *Ça va bien: the Dorcan modern language series* (edited by O A and H M Dobinson, Dorcan Educational, 6 Linley Close, Swindon SN1 4DY, 1989)

> A series of packs for older students (NC years 10 and 11) not studying for GCSE. Titles include: *Bienvenue, En forme, C'est combien?, Bon voyage!* Embodies the supported self-study approach, with the teacher monitoring individual and group work and lending appropriate support as required.

☐ Crossland D and J Ford, *On y va!* (Nelson, forthcoming 1992)
French equivalent of *Pack's an!* (see Fisher, J et al, page 87 for details).

☐ Elston T, N Johns and P McLagan, *K7: le français sur cassette* (Cassell, 1991)
Bank of listening material (based on seven NC Areas of Experience) with supporting activity cards for individual work.

☐ *Eurolab French* (Revilo Language Cards, PO Box 71, Winchester SO23 8VL, 1990)
Comprises 25 x 5 minute audio cassettes, question cards, answer cards and record sheet copymaster. Students select cassettes for independent listening and related activities, and for homework.

☐ Finnie S and A Gray, *Steps to listening: French* (Mary Glasgow, 1992)
Level 1 available. Independent listening practice for first two years of learning French, with supporting worksheets. Instructions on cassettes are in English, to facilitate minimal teacher involvement.

☐ Gray O, *Carte blanche* (Revilo Language Cards, PO Box 71, Winchester SO23 8VL, 1989)
Two sets of reading cards, based on GCSE topics, one Basic, one Higher, and photocopiable record sheets. Pupils can work on their own, and assess their own work.

☐ Gray O, *Carte blanche junior* (Revilo Language Cards, PO Box 71, Winchester SO23 8VL, 1990)
Similar material to the above, intended for third year pupils.

☐ Hertfordshire Achievement Project, *Destination France* (Hertfordshire Achievement Project, 1989 and Egon Publishers Ltd - commercial distributors, 1992)
Modular course for the less able in Years 10 and 11. As far as possible, the materials have precise instructions (written in English) for the pupils, to enable them to work independently and to encourage autonomous learning appropriate to their ability and stage of development. Compatible with GCSE Basic and NC Attainment Targets.

☐ Resources for Learning Development Unit, *Topic-based enrichment materials for independent learning: French* (RLDU, 1981-1988)
Support material for listening and reading practice, pair work and homework for students 11-14.

☐ Velarde E and J Saunders, *A ton casque* (Nelson, 1990)
Material for independent listening practice for GCSE. Can be used on pupils' personal stereos, in class or for homework.

☐ Whelpton T and D Jenkins, *Le monde en face* (Longman, 1990)
'A'/'AS' level material based on recorded interviews. Listening and topic work. Recordings supported by transcripts and language exercises.

Dictionaries

Listed below are three examples of learner dictionaries (French only) which promote the development of independent study skills, at the same time showing what enjoyment can be obtained while broadening one's vocabulary.

☐ *Mini débutants* (Larousse, Paris, 1985-1986) (Distributor: European Schoolbooks, Cheltenham)

    This illustrated dictionary, aimed at younger French pupils, is supported by an exercise book, *Jouons avec les mots,* full of games and tasks which encourage the user to use and enjoy it.

☐ *Maxi débutants* (Larousse, Paris, 1986-1991) (Distributor: European Schoolbooks, Cheltenham)

    Aimed at more advanced French pupils, this 2000-headword volume features thematic illustrations, suitably indexed, and is also supported by an exercise book, *Découvrons le dictionnaire.* This contains, as its cover announces, *150 exercises et jeux pour trouver soi-même les réponses dans le dictionnaire.*

☐ *Collins French pocket dictionary* (Colour edition) (Harper Collins, London, 1990)

    This includes a special section which features a series of wordgames demonstrating how to make the best use of the dictionary. It has been included with the new Collins educational course *Auto,* which places a great emphasis on the encouragement of independent study and student autonomy.

German

☐ Bray B et al, *Mir geht's gut: the Dorcan modern language series* (edited by A O and H M Dobinson, Dorcan Educational, 1989)

    Details as for *Ça va bien* on page 85. Titles include: *Willkommen!, In Form, Was kostet das?, Gute Reise!*

☐ Callaghan S and I Westphal, *Kopfhörer auf!* (Nelson, 1990)

    Details as for *A ton casque,* see Velarde E and J Saunders, page 86.

☐ *Eurolab German* (Revilo Language Cards, 1991)

    Details as for French equivalent, page 86.

☐ Fisher J, *Lesekiste - Collections A and B* (Mary Glasgow, 1986)

    German equivalent of *Bibliobus* (see page 85). Collection A now available on cassette.

☐ Fisher J, V Baker and J Hewett, *Pack's an!* (Nelson, 1991)

    Boxed set of reading cards, arranged by GCSE topics. Three copies each with 48 cards, supported by pupil profiles, teacher's notes and copymasters for extension activities. Complementary resource to enhance mixed ability work in class and for homework.

☐ Gray O, *Kartei* (Revilo Language Cards, 1989)

    Details as for *Carte blanche,* see Gray O, page 86.

☐ Gray O, *Junioren-Kartei* (Revilo Language Cards, 1989)

    Details as for *Carte blanche junior,* see Gray O, page 86.

☐ Resources for Learning Development Unit, *Topic based enrichment materials for independent learning: German* (RLDU, 1988)

    See equivalent French materials on page 86 for details.

☐ Walton C, *Hier steht's* (Mary Glasgow, 1990)
Independent reading practice for first two years of learning German. Similar in style to *A la carte,* see Bougard M T et al, page 85.

Spanish   ☐ Calver M, *A la onda* (Nelson, 1991)
Details as for *A ton casque,* see Velarde E and J Saunders, page 86.

☐ Plymen A M, *A la carta* (Mary Glasgow, 1991)
See *A la carte,* Bougard M T et al, page 85.

Other languages   ☐ Saini H K, *An introduction to Panjabi: a supported self-study course for Panjabi speakers* (H K Saini, 25 Whernside, Wellingborough, Northants NN8 3QQ, 1990)
Material developed with LEA support to enable mother-tongue speakers with limited reading and writing skills in the language to pursue their studies to GCSE.

Adult and Further Education

☐ *Authentik* (Authentik Language Learning Resources Materials Ltd, 27 Westland Square, Dublin 2, Ireland)
A periodical reading and listening resource (five issues a year) for intermediate to advanced students. It consists of a newspaper containing press extracts in the target language, covering a wide range of topics of current interest. Each issue also contains in-depth treatment of one particular topic. Parallel to the newspaper is a cassette containing radio news broadcasts, interviews and features, some specially commissioned, many linked to the newspaper coverage. The package is completed by a *learner's supplement,* printed with the newspaper, which combines a transcript of the recordings with a variety of supplementary activities to exploit the two resources. There is also a separate *Authentik user's guide* available. Versions for **English, French, German** and **Spanish.**

French   ☐ Fournier I, *Breakthrough French study guide, GCSE French: general* and GCSE French (National Extension College, 1984 and 1988)
Material produced by the NEC, a leading correspondence college, to link with Macmillan's *Breakthrough* packages. The first is a brief guide containing unit-by-unit notes and some additional exercises. The latter two are substantial open learning packs which supplement the basic materials to provide for a complete GCSE-by-correspondence course.

☐ Lancashire College, *French dialogues* (Lancashire College for Adult Education)
Material to be used as part of a distance/open learning course offered by the college. Students work on their own then call tutor support as appropriate.

☐ Peltier R and A Corner, *French for you* (Lancashire College, 1992)
May be purchased separately or as part of an open learning course. A more integrated package than the above, incorporating grammar work and other activities.

☐ Pitman Tutorial College/Henley College, *The office SOS kit for French - Course 291* (Pitman Tutorial College, 1990)
   Business French open learning pack for secretaries and receptionists. Incorporates tests which can be assessed as part of optional tutor support available from the two colleges.

☐ **Wakefield College,** *Business French for beginners* (Wakefield District College - open learning language packs, 1992)
   Text plus cassette pack. Students work on the three self-contained units at their own pace, then can book tutor contact for intensive practice.

☐ Fournier I, *Breakthrough German study guide, GCSE German: general* and *GCSE German: extended* (National Extension College, 1984 and 1988)
   Details as for French equivalent, page 88.

German

☐ Mould C, A Yeomans and G Rimmer, *German for you* (Lancashire College, 1992)
   Details as for *French for you,* see Peltier R and A Corner, page 88.

☐ Pitman Tutorial College/Henley College, *The office SOS kit for German - course 290* (Pitman Tutorial College, 1990)
   Details as for French equivalent above.

☐ Wakefield College, *Business German for beginners* (Wakefield District College - open learning language packs, 1992)
   Details as for French equivalent above.

☐ Iglesias Maellas R, C de Osma Calvo and S Truscott, *Spanish for you* (Lancashire College, 1992)
   Details as for *French for you,* see Peltier R and A Corner, page 88.

Spanish

☐ Lancashire College, *Spanish dialogues* (Lancashire College for Adult Education, 1988)
   See French equivalent, page 88.

☐ Lancashire College, *Chinese dialogues, Greek dialogues* and *Portuguese dialogues* (Lancashire College for Adult Education)
   Details as for French equivalent, page 88.

Other languages

☐ Rossi S, *Italian for you* (Lancashire College, 1992)
   Details as for *French for you,* see Peltier R and A Corner, page 88.

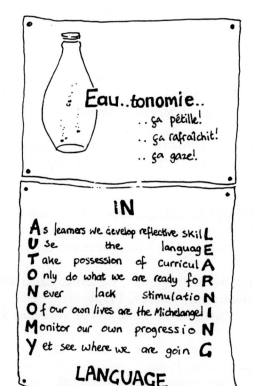